THE OUTDOOR ATHLETE

THE**O**UTDOOR ATHLETE

Total Training for Outdoor Performance

STEVE · ILG

CORDILLERA PRESS, INC.

Publishers in the Rockies

Library of Congress Cataloging-in-Publication Data

Ilg, Steve, 1962-
  The outdoor athlete.

  Bibliography: p.
  Includes index.
  1. Outdoor recreation.   2. Physical education and
training.   I. Title.
GV191.6.I44   1987   796.5   87-13626
ISBN: 0-917895-17-7

Cover photographs of kayaker and cyclist courtesy David Langdon; photographs of climber and skier courtesy Steve Ilg

Cover design by Robert Schram, Bookends, Boulder CO

Typography and design by Shadow Canyon Graphics, Evergreen, CO

Second Edition
    4 5 6 7 8 9

Printed in the United States of America

ISBN: 0-917895-17-7

Cordillera Press, Inc., P.O. Box 3699, Evergreen, Colorado 80439
(303) 670-3010

Contents

Part I:
The Beginning Culmination

Part III:
Exercise Essentials: Training Movements Illustrated

Appendices:
Some Extra Stuff

A Thousand Thanks

To those of you who know me, acknowledgements lie within. These words are as much your energies as mine. I merely collected them for a moment or two. Spirit-specific appreciation is extended to, in no linear order:

Gene Ellis, Joyce and Richard Rossiter, David Langdon, Diane Venuto, Richard and Tina Broida, Anne Preston, Chris Hill, Beverly LeGere, Larry Kishiyama, Coach "Hippety Hop" Jimmy Radcliffe, Dr. Bob Farentinos, Donny Nielsen, Richard Dumais, Johnny Mars, Walter "The Proton Fly" Stasick, Sheila Aguirre, Pat Ament, Gerry Roach, all the members of Fitness Plus Training Facility in Boulder, and to "Apache" (1974-1978), my half-wolf who taught me the most about being a true "Outdoor Athlete."

*I knew they were going to ask me for a dedication.
Geez, I'm really bad at these types of things. . . .*

*To my mom and dad, I guess. After all, they did pay the rent
while I wrote and played outdoors. . . .*

*and to our Mother The Earth, Our Father The Sky,
and to everything and everyone in between.*

"You cannot fly like an eagle with the wings of a wren." —*William Hudson*.

Breeze

Once, while struggling gamely under an overhanging Eldorado crack, my rock-climbing partner Eric, who was physically weaker but more proficient at climbing than I, remarked, "Ilg, you're too strong for your own good!"

Over the years, I have given much thought to that comment. It haunted my budding philosophy concerning outdoor athletics. Indeed, it was that remark which sparked the realization of this book.

In my maturation process since that comment was made, a central question emerged. Are people who are drawn to the more esoteric, individualistic outdoor activities athletes?

Yes.

A dictionary will inform us that an "athlete" is a person who possesses a natural aptitude for physical exercise, like feats of strength, agility, and endurance.

Thus, to be an athlete does not necessarily mandate a soldierlike competitive drive. Be I so bold as to suggest that all beings are athletes? Certainly each of us has at one time displayed these "natural aptitudes for physical exercises." Proof, you ask? Who among us has never been a child? You see, we are all, by little choice of our own, athletes.

And athletes must train. Activity is an instinctual drive. Stagnation is abnormal. It is action — preferably action sought outside society's doors — that is the object of our inner affection and desires.

There are as many theories regarding principles and techniques of modern athletic training as there are individuals to think of them. Some are grandiose. Some are sterile and based on dusty back journals of scientific data. Still others are modest and idiosyncratic. Judgment here, as always, is difficult. At a basic philosophical level, there are no rights and no wrongs, only consequences. It is among this talus of attitudes, perspectives, and ideas that the outdoor athlete must negotiate personal training. Surely, it has been noted, the quickest path to disillusionment is the one blazed by someone else.

In the fabrication of this book, I have had the opportunity to interview, talk, and sometimes escape from lovers of the outdoor world. I needed to know about their preparation for their wilderness endeavors. Or if they prepared at all. Among those who did, each — from casual, recreational enthusiast to devout, multi-sport, hard-core alpinist — conveyed a quaint sense of well-being derived from their training.

Controlled bio-mechanical and physiological studies of outdoor, non-competitive sports are virtually non-existent. The reasons are financial. Unlike "real" athletes who train for competitive purposes, the outdoor athlete brings his skill into the wilderness. Here, no referee or stopwatch records the athletic interplay of the individual and the sport. No real dollars can be made in this arena; the only bucks nearby are the ones with bouncing, white buttocks. Why should high-speed gentility bother with controlled, scientific, and applied economic assistance for these peculiar patrons of the picayune?

This, I think, is best.

In an age of frenzied mass fitness, transitory beliefs, and punk diets, the outdoor athlete has discovered that one impossible thing — a purchase on permanent truth. The outward expression of our inner self in an environment to which we can, as Heraclitus said, "Listen to the essence of things."

Training plays a big part in all of this. Only in training may we finally achieve that inner sanctum of self-rapport that cannot be stolen by a nine-to-five existence. Training resists common analysis, it will forever be a holistic and mercurial experiment of one. It remains an indispensable path to the object of our innermost affection.

"Truth," noted Emerson, "is what works." What you are about

to read is straightforward truth, a consolidation of experiential knowledge based on the trials, errors, and joys of a family. It is my family. Nature makes all men brothers. And so, it is with incestural pleasure that I give you *The Outdoor Athlete.*

A Postscript for the Second Edition

The success of *The Outdoor Athlete* has touched me in many ways. To all of you who have picked up a pen or phone to communicate a feeling, I wish to extend my deep gratitude. The critics have been surprisingly few, and I have done my best to learn from them. Active, positive interest is a quality sadly missing in a world too often bereft of personal character. Again, my many thanks. Have fun, and Tonkahwahkeen, keep your face to the sunshine.

— *Steve Ilg*
  Boulder, Colorado

Part I

The Beginning
Culmination

Sinew

"Physical activity is the cure for most modern ailments."

—Unknown

What is sinew if not the fibrous cement which holds us to our thoughts? As a general introduction to this chapter, I take the opportunity to ask as a friend once asked me, "Are you not plagued from time to time by ridiculous urges, impulses, and longings?" I am.

At times the mystical, almost magical world of the outdoors is so emotionally captivating that vulnerability assists us in shrugging off the real physical demands of nature. Our actions are indeed limitless, spectacular sport.

Unfortunately, though, the player here — the outdoor athlete — all too frequently operates with blinders on. Athletes involved in more orthodox sports train with a good degree of intelligent finesse. It is often painfully evident that the preparatory work of the outdoor athlete is dangerously paradoxical.

Usually, there is no training at all.

To plot the outdoor athlete's attempts at training would be to draw a circle. In lieu of establishing a rising crescendo of performance-enhancing training tables, most outdoor athletes have been content to wallow in a quagmire of haphazard and sporadic "workouts." This is not good, because, as Huxley said: "Nature never overlooks a mistake or makes the smallest allowance for ignorance."

Strength Training

Sport scientists, physiologists, and researchers have struggled for years attempting to categorize and anatomize "strength." The dissection remains inconclusive, but two truths have emerged. The first is that one may be "strong" in many forms. The second is the realization that strength, in any form, comes from within.

The runner has sleek aerobic strength. The cross-country skier possesses an overall endurance-type of strength. The Olympic weightlifter is showy in his explosive strength, while the wily chess master applies mental strength in his art.

Each recognizes that more strength is required to perform better. This necessary insight is usually offered to the outdoor athlete only during self-fashioned crises: flaming out on a strenuous technical rock climb, heaving, weak-kneed up a mountain trail, drooping shoulders hunched from fatigue during a river run. We have all listened — however reluctantly — to that inner voice which speaks up during these times, "I need more strength."

Strength, in whatever form, must become the preeminent tool, a function of one's self which lingers on for seasons waiting to be freed. Strength for the outdoor athlete can only justify its value as a permanent, individual, behavioral trait.

Theodore Roosevelt wrote: "I wish to preach not the doctrine of ignoble ease, but the doctrine of the strenuous life." In athletics in general, and in outdoor sports in particular, one hopes to achieve the doctrine of the strenuous life, with ignoble ease.

Unlike training for more traditional sports, the outdoor world demands more complexity, less fragility. For example, the technical climber experiences a need for powerful, dynamic aerobatics on an overhang. But then he faces a delicate and seemingly holdless wall above. Passage here requires not gross strength, but catlike agility, balance, technique, and controlled muscular tenacity. For

---

. . We have all listened attentively to that inner voice which speaks up during strenuous moments, " I need more strength."

. . . Each strata of the outdoor environment requires a broad base of athletics tempered by specific activity needs.

the back-country skier, exhausting uphill plods are terminated by reflex-demanding downhills brushing snow-laden pine. Each strata of the mountain environment requires broad-based athleticism tempered by specific activity needs.

Gathering Momentum

Strength training means reading both inner and outer language. With each workout comes a lesson. This education often results in a changed perspective toward the way we manage our lives, and our sport.

Getting into a strength training program does not, at times, sound all that inviting. This is especially true for the outdoor athlete. Nature is our preferred playground, our place of worship, and, of course, our gym. The thought of barbells instead of heather makes us malcontent. Knowledge of a summer sun or a snow-locked canyon lurking outside the gym during a scheduled workout time only heightens this feeling. This is natural. Playing hookey from training isn't entirely counterproductive and can occasionally have benefits of its own, including a renewed sense of dedication when one does return to the gym.

But one thing must always be central to the outdoor athlete's training: EFFORT. Make an honest effort at consistent training. As Henry David Thoreau noted, "Most people are not simple enough to believe." That hints that we should reduce the complexity in our lives. Clear thoughts come from unclouded minds. So it is that action, which is training, which in turn is play, takes over. Believe in the daily discipline of a cleansing and intrinsic need.

Strength training must be done in harmony with one's outdoor sport, not in conflict with it. The trick to effectual strength gains

You Can Achieve Whatever Your Mind Believes

lies in a principle called periodzational training. Periodzational training allows effectual workouts by organizing training into a cyclic structure. By an intelligent intermingling of objectives, tasks, and content of training, the outdoor athlete's performance capabilities are enhanced.

Balance. For example, the skier strength trains in the gym during the snowless months. Come winter, a maintenance phase is initiated; here the time spent in the gym is quite low — perhaps one or two times per week. The gym is now a distant second to lots of skiing.

Yet, most people are ruffled by this, and it should not be so. Most people want to "get back into shape" only moments prior to taking to the hills. This erroneous assumption that strength is a transitory event that can be voluntarily captured and manipulated at a whim has led to an ever-increasing amount of foolish accidents and many needless injuries.

Most accidents are a physical manifestation of poor or inadequate preparation. Should grace and awareness momentarily take leave, accidents fill the gap like fat cells lounging where firm muscle fibers ought to be. It is the delicious feeling of strength that offsets and balances the numerous potential pitfalls common to the outdoor sports. In addition to the many physiological benefits which the strength-trained outdoor athlete carries with him into the wilds, strength training accomplishes an improbable goal; it gives one the courage to chase one's star. Training affords us the opportunity to be simple enough to BELIEVE.

Gaining greater strength necessitates some time and a good amount of energy. I understand the difficulty of squeezing mountains, rivers, and snowfields into the structure of our lives — let alone consistent training time. Yet, as with many of the hardships courted in life, it is a cross one must bear. The key is EFFECTIVE training time. This book assumes many of the duties of a professional trainer. It provides the most productive strength training prescription for your time.

Time

The quest for training time has bedeviled all types and calibers of athletes. You are no exception. It is not, however, so much a question of "finding the time," as it is a matter of "*creating* the time" for training. There are no easy answers. You just have to make the time.

Most public gyms remain open at night. If you own a gym, and this can mean a simple barbell set, it stays open all the time. With a little creativity, and by following the suggestions outlined in this book, you can fuse the necessary variables to a successful training regime with tremendous results and little hassle. It just takes a little altering of lifestyle.

Usually, this means a reduction of currently nonproductive, wasted time.

"Time is the formal A PRIORI (or necessary) condition of all appearances whatsoever." — Immanuel Kant.

"Time. That which man is always trying to kill, ends in killing him." — Herbert Spencer.

"The most profitless thing to manufacture is an excuse."
— Unknown.

Over the years, I've listened to many justifications for not wanting to train. In fact, as a personal coach, I have heard some fantastic excuses. Once, for example, a client of mine was ten minutes late for a workout when the telephone rang.

"Uhh, yeah, Steve, it's me, John."

"I know John, I can tell by your voice. Where are you? You're late."

"Listen, I won't be able to make it in today. I'm stuck out here at the airport. Can we reschedule?"

It was a good try, creative and all, but John didn't know that I could see him placing his call from a phone booth across the street.

The bottom line is value. How much value do we attach to our sport? If we REALLY WANT to gain greater strength, enhance outdoor athletic performances, and live all the more meaningfully along the way, we will make the time to train.

Think about this: Many of us have a surprisingly substantial amount of what could be considered "stale time." TV watching is the prime example here. Other examples need not be embellished here, but rather, can be individually contemplated. If you complain about your inadequate strength levels or even general appearance, remind yourself that you fashion your lifestyle — no one else does. Very few of my athletes, for instance, spend more than an hour per day training. Often, much less time than that. This includes not only my recreational fitness clients, but also my world-class, centerfold athletes. By making good use of stale time, the path to greater strength is cleared.

A friend now living in Germany writes: "America has mastered its form of control to such a degree that we don't even need gas chambers any longer . . . they are obsolete in comparison to television and home entertainment centers."

Some young outdoor athletes in Germany.

Space

At a basic level, strength training is not a one-dimensional process. It is simply an element of a much greater athletic wholeness. This holds true for every sport and for every athletic pursuit. In upcoming chapters we shall explore other trainable physiological qualities: Cardiovascular fitness, flexibility, mental skills, and nutrition. Yet despite our massive investment in the academics of the sports sciences, the residual practical applications are roily at best — especially when it comes to strength training. We must reduce the complexities of training and relearn simplicity. Progress is our only teacher. There can be no black and white laws to strength training. What we do depend on, however, is our own reaction to safe and proven sports physiology guidelines. Training must always remain a self-confrontation.

RESISTANCE TRAINING

Weightlifting is a hard sport to pick up. Ultramarathoners, triathletes, ski marathoners, and cyclists train with weights. So, too, do dancers, archers, and martial artists. Resistance training has finally been raised from the paltry barbell-plate-banging consciousness of years past into its now widely respected, if still misunderstood, position. If, as Emerson said so well, "To be great is to be misunderstood," then I nominate resistance training as the greatest of all endeavors. It would appear that the outdoor athlete has confronted the most saturnine monster of indelible visage, when asked to comment about his experience with resistance training. Longstanding myths and old wives tales pepper most peoples' attitudes about lifting resistance for the benefits it bestows upon the body. Technical climbers say that strength-training activities will serve only to add bulk and create inflexibility. Backcountry skiers cite endurance training as all that need be pursued for appreciable training effects. Throw out these calloused and narrow-minded fallacies! Get out of the rigid, old thought patterns and step into the self and collect its ever-abundant harvest. Integrating resistance training into one's life opens channels of energy and thought never before realized.

Here are some highlights of resistance training that encourage all types of athletes to strength train:

- Isolation of specific body parts can be targeted for strength enhancement and injury rehabilitation.

- Each muscle that is trained is also strengthened at its attachments.

- A more efficient fatigue-toxin removal system is acquired.

- A progressive, monitorable atmosphere is possible.

- Results vary according to the prescription.

- Properly done resistance training stresses muscles, not joints.

- Consistent resistance training improves neuromuscular pathway efficiency.

- Nutrition is inherent to strength-training philosophy.

- An increase in self-confidence and physical ability is manifested through progress.

Gathering Form

"Grace," wrote LaRochefoucauld, "is to the body what clear thinking is to the mind." No better wisdom can be given to an athlete.

I am a stickler for elegance. It is more important to me to have an athlete strength train in elegant form and lift less poundage than it is to herald the weightlifter who lifts Herculean tonnage but does so in less than poetic form. My philosophy, although it may be difficult on one's ego, is by far safer, and the training effect greater.

If the end result of any pursuit remains a fixed entity, failure, in one form or another, is certain. The goal, if there is such a thing, for the outdoor athlete is never fitness. Health assumes a leechlike disposition that follows us everywhere. Although its presence is continually felt, recognized, and revelled in, the outdoor athlete seldom chases it. He or she is far too concerned about the wisp of cloud moving above or too absorbed in perfecting uphill ski technique in the crystalline snow beneath than to be bothered by the clinical aspects of what he or she is doing. This is a strange thing. Fitness comes unbidden to the outdoor athlete. This runs cross-grain to conventional thought which seems to say, "To attain fitness you must embark on a purposeful journey and never, ever lose sight of your goal."

The difference between the rest of the world's attempts at fitness and ours can be seen in the analogy of kite-flying.

There are two ways to fly a kite, the Eastern way and the Western

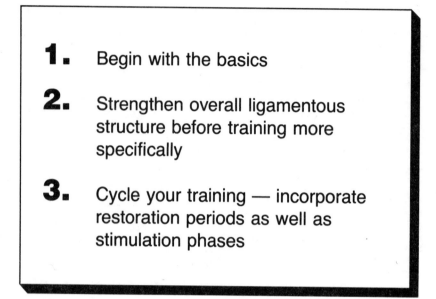

1. Begin with the basics

2. Strengthen overall ligamentous structure before training more specifically

3. Cycle your training — incorporate restoration periods as well as stimulation phases

way. The Westerner, seeing what a fine day it is, gathers his kite and spool, hikes to his favorite field, and immediately runs very hard, letting the kite out behind him. After several tries and much heavy breathing, the kite has taken to the air. The Easterner, sensing what a fine day it is for kite flying, packs his kite, spool, and a reading book and heads off to his favorite field. A while later, a stiff breeze interrupts his reading, so he sets his book down, pits his back against the breeze, and gently releases his kite high into the air.

Sometimes, you see, less effort creates more results. My approach will give you the economy of exercise prescription. Your kite will never fly higher.

It may be hard for me to convince the active naturalist that there is substance to lifting. Its beauty is sometimes masked by the intimidating sneer of the weights and machines. To get beyond that, one must use concentration as a vehicle. Elegant form and concentration become one's ignitors for consistent, strength-gaining workouts. Once this is achieved, the quaint pulchritude of the weight room grows addictive. Beware, at advanced stages, lifting transcends itself and becomes a kind of organized spirituality that lies above technique, sets and reps, and poundages.

Resistance training wears many faces. Long ago the Greek wrestler, Milo, toted around a calf as his weight-training endeavor. As the calf grew, so did Milo's strength. Later, rock replaced cows (fortunately), and then iron replaced rocks. Our selection today is vast: Cable machines, barbells, dumbbells, cam-type machines, variable-resistance machines, pneumatic machines, etc., etc. Which is the best? Which is most effective over the long run? Which best serves the skier? . . . the climber? . . .

Machines or Free Weights?

I hold to an axiom: Machines should be used as a supplement TO, rather than a substitute FOR, free weights.

Free weights cater to the fundamental and diverse needs of the outdoor athlete. Usage of free weights requires total body integration. This neuromuscular element is neglected in machine-only training. Empirical evidence shows that machines do not fit everyone perfectly. This may cause joint irritations, some subtle, others substantial. Free weights allow diversity in hand placements, foot stances, etc. One's body is allowed to make natural adjustments and biomechanical compensations for potentially negative stress points. This versatility can be regulated to prevent, overcome, and rehabilitate micro-traumas and other injuries.

Perhaps most essential to the reader of this book is the coordination and interplay brought about by free weight training. Multiple muscular movements through better directional control appeal to our bodies' neurological and neuromuscular systems. We begin to reach within our bodies and discover a well-spring of physical and emotional talent. This is true training.

Football coach Al Vermiel had his own answer to the free-weights versus machine question. He said, "I've never seen an athlete play the game sitting down." Ahh . . . such insight!

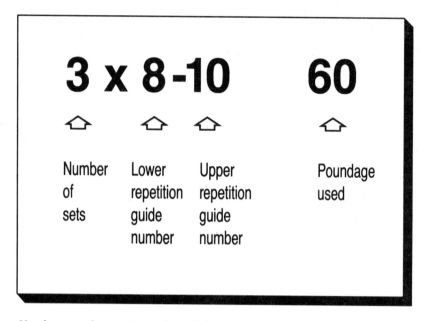

Numbers are the vertebrae of strength training.

The Numbers Game

Numbers make up the vertebrae of strength training. Yet, it is not the numerical superiority in pounds that hallmarks a great lifter. Remember, elegance at all times. Bombastic performance yields only injuries and a close-minded ignorance to the real chord of weight training. The importance lies not only in the sets and repetitions, but in muscular failure, proper recovery, and the liberation of one's mind into the body.

To make optimal use of training time, the outdoor athlete changes his mindset from alpinist to strength trainer. He must become familiar with basic strength-training principles. Enter: THE PROGRESSIVE OVERLOAD PRINCIPLE. This is the golden rule of strength training. It is also the one most often neglected. This principle states that each workout, in some manner (recovery time, weight, or tempo), must be greater than the previous one. Muscles are resilient. One must really force them to respond. Upon initiation of a routine, the beginner may notice large leaps in progress. These "hypertrophic adaptations" soon plateau. This initial strength increase has been linked to what some sports scientists refer to as "maximum neural activations." After about four weeks, these learning-induced neural gains peak out, hence the introduction of more advanced training techniques is necessary.

The following is a description of how the overload principle is commonly applied in the gym.

3x10-12
3 is the number of sets
10 is the lower repetition guide number
12 is the higher repetition guide number

The resistance that is lifted (a barbell, dumbbell, Nautilus machine, cow, whatever) must cause one to reach momentary muscular failure — the point at which one cannot (in good form) lift the resistance any more — by 12. That was set number 1. Thus, momentary muscular failure, it can be said, dictates the end of EACH set. After failure has been reached, a between-sets rest has been earned. This rest is usually limited to 45 seconds. Begin set number 2 immediately afterward. Let us say that on set number 2, we could only lift the resistance for 11 repetitions before failure was reached. Rest again. By the third and final set, muscular fatigue contributes to our inability to reach 12 repetitions. We could only crank out 9 reps. That's fine. Say that we have been using 70 pounds during all of this. We must stay at 70 pounds until we can accomplish ALL THREE SETS AT 12 REPETITIONS. After that glorious day, the poundage is increased. In doing this, a whole new workload must be met and overcome once again.

Manipulation of the set/rep scheme is the key to unlocking greater strength gains in many capacities. The following is a generalization of how different set and rep schemes influence physiological results in the muscle:

Sets and Reps	Result
4x6-8	Most suitable for achieving bulk and high levels of strength and power.
3-4x10-12	Significant strength gains with less cellular proneness to bulk.
3-4x20-?	Endurance-oriented strength and stamina. Has shown an ability to increase cardiovascular fitness.

I recommend training in all three "zones" at one time or another. Continual performance of the same set and rep scheme may offer a "pumped" sensation in the muscle. Do not, however, confuse a "pump" with "progress." Mix it up. Do not shy away from heavy weights. I have attributed much of the success of endurance athletes to a logical integration of lower repetitions (heavy weights) during a seasonal strength prescription. Abandonment of heavy strength training retards potential.

Many cross-purposes exist in training. Too often, athletes — particularly young athletes wishing to outperform aging predecessors — are quick to forego trivial matters such as basic training. When I first started writing articles concerning basic training for outdoor athletes, my readership responded. Negatively. Blinded by the logic of holistic training, they craved only sport-specific exercises: "What will make me ski better?" "Climb harder?" "Ascend more peaks with less effort?" My urges for a more balanced and fundamental approach to training left them with a pensive distaste. This, they wrote to me, is going backward, not forward! Yet it is the manufacture and application of extreme program designs that lead most alpinists astray. It is only the most sagacious that realize the meaning of the proverb, "To go forward, you first must go backward."

Most of us do not have sufficient basic training to be jumping into the advanced stages of training. The line separating advanced, productive training and injury is a fine one. With dismay I've found myself in the position of having to tell a former non-subscriber, "I hate to tell you so, but, I told you so." They nod their acknowledgement as their injured shoulder hangs limply at their side. If one must train energetically, map out a systematic, progressive plan — a master plan.

Mind to Muscle Link

In later chapters, sport-specific training suggestions abound. Many are advanced. Emerson wrote that "nothing great was ever achieved without enthusiasm." I agree. Elegant technique, however, must temper all enthusiasm in any program. Before advanced sport-specific training becomes effective, one must fully develop what has roughly been referred to as the "mind-to-muscle link." It is this link that is the alleviator of training boredom and stagnation. It is this mystical, elusive "link" that is the omnipresent current of feeling that unites results and goals.

To a number of thinkers, this mind-to-muscle link concept is an unnecessary vein of thought. For example, many Eastern religions and philosophies regard the entire human being as one being, with no delineation between mind, body, or spirit. It was Rene Descartes, the French mathematician of "I think therefore I am" fame, who forced a mechanistic division of the mind from the body. I believe it is a wonderful thing that strength-training practice presses us to return to a living spirit using all energies of nature. As we lift a weight and are tested to our "limits," the body can respond only by a fusion of mind, body, and spirit.

During your next workout, contemplate this:

There is subtle technique to every movement. Indeed, every moment. Take note of a ballerina. Or of the martial artist. Observe their economy of motion. How they hold themselves, shoulders back, heads held high, open to nature. They are off their hips, not sunk into them. They float with the earth's movement and flow with the gentle tug of gravity. One can spot these breathing statues of beauty in a multitude of more lazy mortals. The master athlete — who as Dan Millman has taught us in his wonderful book *The Peaceful Warrior* is the athlete who brings his sport into each of

The "Mind-to-Muscle Link" is an elusive but omnipresent current of feeling that unifies results and goals. *Photo by Diane Venuto.*

life's moments — is the role model of the public. Strength training may be the best way to start feeling our natural self, to discover again the child within us. It begins, of course, with practice.

Each repetition in the gym contains two distinct phases, a powerful and explosive "positive" phase, and a slower, more controlled "negative" phase. Technically, the positive phase occurs when the muscle belly SHORTENS during contraction. The negative phase occurs when the muscle belly LENGTHENS as tension develops in the muscle. The phases are linked with rhythm, no jerkiness here. Elegance, always. Become that muscle or muscle group that you are training. Discover where your energy is and connect it to that body part. Tempo, tempo. A piston moving methodically up and down. Push the muscle to failure. Nothing else matters in the whole world but that set, those reps. When you fail, fail elegantly; never "cheat" the resistance up by using extraneous movements. Breathing should come naturally, usually with the exhalation married to the positive phase.

Each repetition in the gym contains two distinct phases which must be linked by rhythm . . . Remember: Elegance always.

Like any relationship, this synergism must be worked at, dogmatically, day after day. It is with this newly developed form of consciousness that our sport soon becomes technically and physically easier to perform. Keep your strength within your life, learn how to make your strength-training workout a masterpiece in self-artistry.

Then you will be ready for the greatest joy of all, the fusing of this elegance into your sport.

Advanced Training Techniques

SuperSets: This technique involves choosing two exercises to be performed consecutively, then taking the between-set rest. Three exercises done in this manner are called TriSets. More than three exercises are called GiantSets.

Pre-Exhaustion Sets: Here, a body part is isolated by a more specific exercise before being coerced to partake in a more general exercise. For illustration, to pre-exhaust the frontal thigh, do three sets of twelve to fifteen reps in the leg extension, then do three sets of eight to ten reps in the back squat.

Descending Sets: Also known as "The Stripping Method." The objective of descending sets is to keep the lifter one step ahead of momentary failure by reducing the resistance as failure approaches. This is one of my favorite tools. Descending sets stress many physiological aspects of muscle function.

Break-Away Sets: At least that is what I call them. To be done with weighted pullups or dips, Break-Aways work the following way. Upon failure with the added weight, simply discard the burden and "go for it" at pure body weight. Incredibly fatiguing, this outstanding technique is unparalleled for acquisition of muscle stamina.

Power Training: The Secret of a Lifetime

Envision for a moment the ensuing fictional rock-climbing scenario:

Mr. Glippy, forty feet above his protection, is clinging to a fingertip edge while trying to "get a piece in." Five minutes and three-quarters of his rack later, Mr. Glippy's maxed-out forearms finally rebel. A questionable but feasible handhold beckons two feet above his head. Glippy eyes the "bucket." Sewing machine leg has, by this time, attacked not one, but both of Glippy's lower limbs. Unbeknownst to him, Mr. Glippy's subconscious has already been placed on "Red Alert," prepared for the task at hand. Far below, onlookers shield their eyes from the white glare of Glippy's knuckles. At long last, Glippy goes for it, lunging. He makes the move and lives.

STRENGTH enabled Mr. Glippy to hang on, but POWER was responsible for the lunge to success.

Perhaps the greatest derivative of strength training is POWER. Power differs from strength. Power is the sum of a physiological algebraic equation: Power = Strength x Speed.

Emerson sensed this concept long ago. "In skating over thin ice," he wrote, "our safety is in our speed."

The gorilla is strong. The cat is powerful. To touch true power is to learn the essence of practical strength.

Power training's value lies in its volitional development. Power training produces neuromuscular interplay and disentangles poor motor skill control. This weaving of volitional and mechanical control produces balance, coordination, and agility.

Basically, we know that power is very valuable for any athlete; however, sports scientists just don't know the exact biological intricacies which give birth to power. I believe much of my success

Ilg demonstrating the concept of power: *Left:* Start position of the Power Dip; *Right:* Top position.

with athletes can be directly attributed to power. It is instrumental in the freeing of an athlete's natural ability. If your physiological curiosity beckons and you wish a more cerebral look into the physiology of power, I recommend *Plyometrics: Explosive Power Training* by James C. Radcliffe and Bob Farentinos, Ph.D. (Human Kinetics Publishers).

To achieve power, we can employ special exercises such as powercleans, power pulls, and plyometric training (jumping- and hopping-related exercises stressing the fast-twitch muscle fibers). Additionally, power is attained by the attentive application of the positive phase in regular strength-training workouts.

The muscularly "weak" athlete, therefore, discovers a new friend in power. Power, remember, depends on speed, not just strength.

POWER FOR OUTDOOR ATHLETES

Backpackers and General Mountaineers: Legs and hips,

developed through power training, become more effective as a driving force for uphill travel. Subsequent linkage of power generated through the lower body is passed through the midsection and, finally, to the arms. This overall effect creates a much needed arm carriage and contributes to a machinelike proficiency for the non-technical alpinist.

Backcountry and Alpine (Downhill) Skiers: The skier's power is also generated by the buttock or gluteal region. Although the skier has the assistance of skis beneath him, power training can reduce fatigue while creating faster uphill movement. Concurrently, a more coordinated and controlled downhill technique is often discovered after a season of power training. Vital to telemarkers and Alpine skiers, power training improves the reaction time of sensory to motor pathways.

Technical Climbers and Whitewater Athletes: Power is rapidly accelerating the potential of these athletes. Power training increases upper and lower body awareness; this kinesthesia cognizance quickens reaction time and sharpens overall motor control. Female climbers concerned with muscular strength should cherish power training because of the independent but catalytic effect it has on strength.

Mountain Bikers: For the cyclist attracted to raw terrain, "dynamic balance" must move from concept to innate quality. As the mature mountain biker increases his or her level of difficulty, control of the body during constant balance point changes is a must. No matter how many more gears or other performance enhancing accoutrements high technology hands us, there comes a point where mechanics offer nothing and athletic ability everything. Manipulation of the most difficult and the most satisfying terrain mandates neuro-muscular artistry. If you do not power train, you sacrifice control in crucial balance point situations.

Until recently, outdoor athletes shunned the dimension of power. The concept of speed in movements was intangible, unnecessary. In the early 1970s, a Colorado rock climber named Steve Wunsch literally exploded many conceptions of technical climbing, and, in retrospect, power. In a leaping, aeronautic ascent of the Kloberdanz Roof in Eldorado Canyon, Wunsch cast forth new athletics into climbing. A race to learn had begun. Though his example was quite theatrical, more subtle but no less dramatic benefits of power can be realized by every outdoor athlete.

The more training experiences we can draw from, the more balanced we perform. Power, the great salvager of strength, percolates within our being, waiting.

Respiration

"Wealth, I ask not; hope nor love. Nor a friend to know me.
All I ask; the heaven above, and the road below me."

—*Robert Louis Stevenson*

Cardiovascular (CV) training brings the body into optimal condition. It intensifies our fitness. CV training can lead one to finely printed and enthused inner motivation. At times, it is that long solitary run which remains the only cure-all to life's difficulties. Uncannily, between footfalls and exhales, the extended CV session moderates pandemonium and strife.

Metabolic needs dictate the type and degree of cardiovascular and cardiorespiratory (CR) fitness. A hiker's need for CV fitness differs from that of the technical climber. Some of the benefits of CV-CR conditioning follow. Envision their effect.

- Enhances the oxygen transportation system.

- Accelerates the removal of lactic acid and other fatigue toxins after a workout or outing.

- Remains the only way to liberate stored body fat tissue effectively.

- Increases the capacity to store glycogen and phosphogens (the body's intrinsic energy sources).

- Increases the aerobic capacity of skeletal muscle.

- Enhances the oxygenation of carbohydrates and fats.

- Improves heart and lung capacity and blood pressure.

- Contributes to an elevated sense of well-being.

- Allows for solitary time for self-focusing of goals.

CV Training Methods

Stark differences split alpinists' postures toward aerobic workouts. One summer, I recall making a first ascent of a distant Flatiron satellite rock formation above Boulder with Gerry Roach. Downtown, I queried him as to the location of the tower. The Everest summiteer brushed the question aside, waving an all-encompassing hand into the backdrop, "Up there a piece." Not bothering to DRIVE nearer to the approach, we began hiking. Well, Gerry was hiking. I was sprinting at about 70 percent intensity. The stride length of this tall, soft-spoken, angular man must be fifteen feet. At least. It was a quintessential mountaineer's climb — an unending, rigorous uphill approach interrupted by a moderate technical climb maybe two pitches in length. This was followed by a mandatory circumnavigation of the tower to "scope out" other first ascent route possibilities. Finally, a return at break-neck speed via a "trail" which didn't exist.

As there are guidelines to strength training, so, too, are there ducts connecting one's response to CV training. I use the phrase, CV training, to mean exertion which stresses one's heart and, resultantly, the vascular system. Many incorrectly use the term "aerobic

Gerry Roach on Flatiron climb near Boulder. *Photo, Ilg archives.*

activity" to mean cardiovascular training. Aerobic activity is CV training done AT MODERATE INTENSITY but FOR LONGER DURA-TIONS. CV training, which stresses both upper and lower body, results in greater energy (caloric) expenditure. Those wishing to reduce body fat levels should keep this point in mind.

One trick for fat loss is to allow the body to reach a definite fat-metabolism stage, usually around twenty-five minutes of consistent aerobic exertion, then increase the caloric demand on the body. This results in a larger net gain of calories being spent from fat deposits. It works. I use this simple but effective principle often with many people.

Whatever one's chosen aerobic activity — jogging, swimming, cycling, etc. — the following techniques help achieve a more pro-fitable overall aerobic training effect:

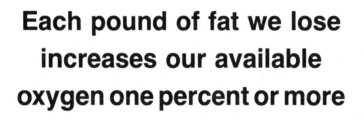

Each pound of fat we lose increases our available oxygen one percent or more

LSD

This is the long, slow, overdistance concept. This method prioritizes duration and time rather than intensity. Unmatched for attaining an aerobic base capacity. Word of caution: LSD is hard on joints and mind. Use discretion when implementing LSD into training regimes. Sample LSD workout: six to eighteen miles (or forty-five to ninety minutes) at conversation-paced intensity.

FARTLEK TRAINING

This is a poorly named but highly regarded form of aerobic training. This technique calls for the sporadic inclusion of "surges" while maintaining the elevated heart rate. The manipulation of the surges varies the intensity and the results of the workout. Examples of Fartlek training on a stationary cycle:

Begin workout by cycling at moderate intensity for twenty mi-

CV Training done in moderate workloads appears to be the optimal choice for ridding oneself of bodyfat.
Photo by Clay Patzer.

nutes. Every ten minutes thereafter, increase pedal cadence and/or increase wheel resistance setting to high. Hold for three to eight minutes. Return to moderate intensity. Continue as desired.

CV SUPERSETS

This procedure is good for those who find aerobic training tedious or monotonous. Here, one alternates one form of aerobic activity with another, interchanging as desired. An indoor example:

Begin the workout with fifteen minutes of stationary cycling. Get off. Run and get a jump rope. Jump (try tricks for coordination) for ten minutes. Stop, then get on the bike again. Repeat this process until moist (the longer the better). If one wishes, introduce another "prop" into the scheme (aerobic tri-sets). Addition of more "props" is called aerobic giant-sets. Be creative.

In a less technical vein, consider this. Hang around the local high school or college. Each day cross-country, ski, and track teams offer fantastic workouts. Join in.

CV conditioning presents the outdoor athlete with more than just the gift of merely huffing and puffing less than non-training partners. It solidifies the body of one's spirit and energy, and, as Blake noted, "Energy is eternal delight."

The Cardiovascular Training Effect

"We should approach running not as if we were trying to smash our way through some enormous wall, but as a gentle pastime by which we can coax a slow continuous stream of adaptations out of the body." — Researcher Hans Frederick.

Mr. Frederick's outlook should be considered for all active pursuits. Tread with care. Balance aerobic training with other fitness activities. Gains in aerobic training come, yet they are tethered by two predominant factors, age and current fitness level. The greatest training effects occur during puberty. As childhood blends into adulthood, the CV-CR training effect becomes harder to achieve. Let's face it, at age fourteen, we are at our animal best.

CV training can be addictive. This is supported by science. I recall my own endorphin-induced fanaticism. Each week I HAD to catalog my ninety miles. The benefits at this work level are arguable. Dr. Fred Hatfield, a world-record holder in powerlifting, offers sage advice for any athlete caught up in this go-for-broke frame of mind. ". . . you are not interested in the rather abstract and often arbitrary standards that are applied when you are talking about general health. The operative questions for you are: 'Does this make me a better competitor?' and 'How much do I need?' "

CV fitness ends at three workouts a week, each for forty minutes. Above this workload, one needs to make a philosophical choice: Am I training for fitness or something else? Moderate workloads or joint-endangering higher volumes? The choice is yours.

It seems funny to me, I receive more questions concerning minimal or maintenance requirements for aerobic fitness than I do questions concerning improvement of aerobic capacity! Are we so fit as to forego improvement and be content with our current condition? Has our pinnacle of ultimate aerobic potential already been established? Never have I found this to be true. Nor will I ever, I should think.

The lasting effects of CV training are still being researched. Theories and speculations flourish. I believe one thing MUST be accepted. As one's CV fitness increases, it becomes more difficult to achieve greater gains. Therefore, I see it imperative for the athlete to:

1. Establish a critical body composition and attain a bodyweight/bodymass ratio most efficient to his sport, and

2. Structure all CV training to maintain that level.

Discover the minimal amount of CV training which maintains effective respiratory and bodymass states. Attempt balances here. Anything more, and the outdoor athlete has shifted his athletic priorities elsewhere.

Cardiovascular Training Devices

It's easy to "blow-off" CV training. It is hard work that necessitates an appreciable chunk of time. Dismissal of aerobic training can only be justified by injury or illness. Death is also an acceptable excuse, I guess. Otherwise, it is crucial to find the time. Running has an important movement pattern for the reader of this book, and it comes recommended. If one finds running distasteful or too severe on the joints, other avenues exist: Jumping rope, swimming, stationary cycling, or bicycling. Find something that is enjoyable. Brisk walking (don't laugh) is quite good and is nontraumatic on joints. Included below are a few unique aerobic training alternatives with which I have had good experiences.

ROLLER SKIING

Dry-land skiing. Skiing on wheels. Excellent upper and lower

body conditioner, improves cardiovascular and muscular strength. Fun and exciting. A tad expensive. Check out local road and ordinance conditions before purchasing these skis.

ROLLER BLADES[1]

My personal favorite. Skates with wheels in lieu of blades. A rapturous and innovative approach. Superb calorie burner and overall conditioner with the extra confluence of reflexology . . . these things have no brakes. Skating and skiing technique are stunningly simulated. Might replace coffee as an early morning pick-me-up. Same ordinance warning as with roller skiing.

NORDICTRAC[2]

This stationary ski machine is perhaps the most plausible of all indoor exercisers. A hearty stamp of approval. Immune to poor weather and exceedingly sane on the joints. Not so sane on the pocketbook.

VERSACLIMBER[3]

An exceptional apparatus. A vertical treadmill for all fours. The general alpinist could not make a wiser investment. Make it a point to get on one soon. Ideal for mountaineers who encounter much low-angle climbing. A weighty expense is the singular drawback.

VersaClimber.
Photo courtesy of
Heart Rate, Inc.

---

[1]RollerBlades are available from North American Sports Training, 9700 W. 75th Street, Suite T, Minneapolis, MN 55344 (1-800-328-0171).

[2]NordicTrac: PSI, 141 WS Johnathan Blvd., N. Chaska, MN 55318.

[3]VersaClimbers. For more information contact Heart Rate, Inc. 3186-G Airway Ave. Costa Mesa, CA 92626. (714) 850-9716 Outside CA (800) 237-2271.

Recovery and Suppleness

"There is no such thing as overtraining. There is only undereating, undersleeping, and failure of will."

— The Barbarian Brothers

"Man must be stretched. If not in one way, then another."

— William James

Many athletes jeopardize their training by . . . training. Overstress is counterproductive to the training concept and is a mark of the immature athlete. More effort is not always wise. Recuperation. Think about it.

"Macho" athletes become ignorant when the time arrives to consider giving the body its much needed rest. They tend to believe that resting is for "wimps" and "only the weak cannot work through injuries or plateaus." To rely on such pasty advice is not sound, productive logic. That same sophomoric macho man can usually be found weeks, months, or years later . . . chronically injured, unable to perform.

Training is a continuing process of self-examination. It is an open communication between judgment and dedication. The best athletes achieve this inner rapport through patience. The novice, abandoning judgment for immediate gratification, fails at this perception and always, in one way or another, falls short of potential.

I recall an early student of mine. Nick, you see, was a boxer. At seventeen and introverted, Nick needed an outlet. His dad gave him a membership to my gym. I gave him boxing.

The first thing I noticed about Nick was his heart. He had a heart bigger than the Himalaya and a thousand times warmer. He responded to the training quickly like many. As baby fat receded and muscle grew, in his eyes began to shine a visionary luminescence. I'd seen this before.

Though his heart was large, Nick's athleticism left much to be desired. He couldn't jab and he always turned his head. Footwork eluded him and his nose bled easily. Yet, I had instilled a sport in him, and the image of a heavy bag consistently swung from the rafters of his mind. He couldn't train enough. He wanted a fight. He wanted to make his dad proud.

My apprehension grew as his training days lengthened. Tirelessly he would slug away at the weights, the roads, and the 'bag.'

"Nick," I spurted forth one day, "you gotta take it a little easier, we've got time . . ."

"Nah, I'm okay. Oh, I meant to tell you, I joined this other boxing team, they're gonna work me out, too."

I watched as Nick's body began to feed upon itself. It needed the energy to keep his Himalayan heart and soul alive. Before Nick's first match I taped his gloves on him between twinges of apprehension. Nick's eyes, once filled with illusions of grandeur, were now full of fear. Nick's dad, ringside, rubbed his palms to and fro. There was a crowd, too, small but potent.

The bell rang. Nick's opponent rushed forth and threw a jab. Nick turned away from the punch (of course) and blocked it with his nose. An official time-out was called because of blood. The fight was slow and piggish with much plodding and weighty breathing. Sometime in the third round, the ref called the match. Nick had kissed the canvas too many times.

I saw Nick the other day, the first time in a long while. He wore

A fine line exists between peak condition and overstress. The rest is up to you.

Paul Ernst and sequoia on a High Sierra siesta.

a weary physique, tall and thin, beardy and disheveled. Nick had quit boxing. Had to. Got injured, he said, "a shoulder." I helped him pack a bag of groceries — that was his job. Nick, the champion, had flamed out. An overzealous warrior beaten by his own sword. I wish now that it hadn't been my donation that had started his battle.

Be cautious when mapping out starry-eyed training objectives. It is when one is feeling most healthy and alive that alertness must be increased. A fine line exists between peak condition and over-stress.

Hearing Inner Messages

If training done with maximum intensity is unproductive, three clues may indicate possible problem areas:

1. The training is intense enough to stimulate strength, but the training volume is too great. This causes the body to use all its reserves to overcome the effects of the workout with too little left over for gains.

2. Besides training too long, the training might be occurring too frequently. Lack of adequate sleep falls under this possibility.

3. Nutrient intake may be insufficient for cellular tissue maintenance or growth.

All training incurs stress, and stress is cumulative. At times, particularly in strength training, this effect is dramatic. Muscles become pumped, then sore. They are recuperating. So let them. For about two days. Denser muscle tissues such as the lower back may need longer recovery periods. Train with the body, not against it. Do not beat the body into oblivion. The highest caliber athletes (and those who have been around the longest) train unbelievably hard. Then they step back. Recovering. Stronger, they return and push again, harder.

Do the "Splits"

There are two phases to all training, a STIMULATIVE PHASE and a RESTORATION PHASE. The former is a high-intensity period, the latter an acknowledgement to the body's call for cellular repair and growth. Physical strength comes, oddly enough, during rest. To insure continued gains without the chance of overtraining, we rely upon SPLIT ROUTINES. Here is a sampling:

Sample Split Routine A

day one
    strength train chest, shoulders, triceps

day two
> strength train back, biceps, forearms, calves

day three
> strength train thighs, abdominals

day four
> do long sessions of flexibility/CV training

Sample Split Routine B

day one
> strength train upper body

day two
> strength train lower body

day three
> do long sessions of flexibility/CV training

Sample Split Routine C

day one
> strength train full body

day two
> CV training: aerobic, long distance

day three
> do sport specific or kinesthetic training

day four
> do flexibility and mental skill training

Maintaining an effective, creative, and changing split routine is

Maintaining an effective and creative training program is a challenge to our adaptive potential. *Photo by Rob Woolf.*

a challenge to the body's adaptive potential. When done intelligently, split routines greatly decrease the likelihood of overtraining and injury. Training plateaus will dwindle in the eye of progression's fury.

Suppleness

Take notice of the inclusion of flexibility training in the above schemes. As one gains strength, a degree of intra-muscular tension is created. This can cause muscles to tighten and grow taut. Such pressure limits athletic mobility and works against the value of strength enhancement.

Flexibility is sly. It is more than muscle elasticity or limp ligaments. It is an elaborate and on-going sensitivity to the athletic environment. It is, in fact, a responsiveness to the demands of activity.

Inflexibility does not come naturally. As toddlers, we were supple. No need to allot time for stretching sessions back then! What happened? We "grew up," that's what. The socialization process that urges us into the "real world" comes packaged with a lot of stress. Unfortunately, muscles tend to act as a net, capturing all sorts of perceived fears and tensions begotten from daily living.

How do experts value suppleness?

Christian Giffith, technical rock climber: "For mantles (a type of climbing maneuver) and complicated gymnastics, arm flexibility is a precondition. On steep and overhanging rock where finger power is at a premium, if you have to have legs at all, it is a necessity that they are supple enough to use.

Alpinist Michael Morrissey: "In my mind, flexibility is more important than strength."

Flexibility is more than limp ligaments; it is a living sensitivity to the demands of an athletic life. *Photo by Beverly Legere, from Ilg archives. Model, Joyce Rossiter.*

Technically, there are two types of flexibility, dynamic and static. Dynamic flexibility refers to the resistance of joints to motion. A cat demonstrates great dynamic flexibility if the feline has the misfortune of being dropped from a height. Very efficiently the cat recoils, tumbles, and regains balance. No damage has been incurred because of the cat's remarkable suppleness.

More familiar is "static" flexibility. This means the range of motion about a joint. A more poetic definition mixes Eastern philosophy with Western pragmatism: Static flexibility is a state, an openness, a harmonious relaxation of our inner mechanics.

The outdoor athlete requires flexibility for the same reason he needs strength training — joint health. Enter a word here: Proprioceptive. This voluminous word refers to the impulses of tendons, ligaments, and muscles. As one performs outdoor activities, great force is generated among the cordlike sinews connecting bones. The athlete with flexible and strong joints has the physiological advantage of calloused joint health. This decreases negative inhibitory responses which normally restrict range of motion.

Attaining suppleness starts by accommodating the pain of stretching. The pain is a sweet agony from within; it guides. Follow it without alarm. The joints, elated by our attempt to free them, respond with daggers of smarting delight. Look into this pain and relax. Do not force any movement. To be supple takes time and effort, but it is highly rewarding, both mentally and physically.

Practical Flexibility

There is a simple, enthralling thing about flexibility. Looseness is a state that can be achieved by holding static postures over long periods of time. Practical flexibility dives deeper and touches the spirit. Practical flexibility training means balancing and counterbalancing a variety of forces. Practical flexibility provides supple, vigorous musculature with clear neural pathways. The ability to move a joint freely — and poetically — necessitates flexibility movements united with kinesthetic movements.

Consider the following for a beginning: Perform standing one-legged positions, then movements during static flexibility training. With practice, do a one-legged squat and note the call of practical flexibility. Don't be discouraged; just keep practicing. If your knees hurt, get into the gym and strength train on one of the programs in this book for a few months, then try again.

During your next strength training session, hold a light barbell overhead. Now, slowly descend to a bottom position of a back squat, and return to start position. Take thirty seconds to perform one repetition. Now do three to five reps. Note the interplay of practical flexibility and strength.

Supple Body, Clear Mind

Flexibility sessions should clear the mind of clouded thoughts and perceived troubles. Remember, flexibility is more than mere stretching. For the outdoor athlete, it is a self-evolving state. It needs to be nurtured often and as a separate, vital component in the training spectrum, not as a casual warm-up or cool-down.

Nutrition

We are our nutrients. The reflection of dietary intake is felt and seen in daily performance, sport or otherwise. The effects are extensive and complex. There can be short-term, flamboyant consequences and there can be long-term, subtler displays. There can be beneficial or detrimental effects. The choice is ours. The experiment never ends.

For optimal vitality, awareness, and durability of our being, we must take in those nutrients that are most essential. Think simplicity. Make each nutrient count. The athlete is concerned with six types: Carbohydrates, fats, proteins, water, vitamins, and minerals.

Fats

Most of us are conditioned to and fall prey to random urges for unneeded foods. These "treats" are usually fat-infested. More than half of us will die from fat-burdened arteries caused because of our "moderate indulgences." This must stop. For the athlete, it must stop now. There is an apt, albeit unknown quote: "Death is nature's way of telling you to slow down."

Per molecule, fats contain less oxygen than any other nutrient.

FATS

A very complex molecule —
   the body is reluctant to metabolize fats.
In weight bearing sports, bodyfat
   hinders performance.

Examples
Oils • Salad dressings • Sauces • Butter

CARBOHYDRATES

"Simple" or "complex" refers to the
molecular structure of the carbohydrate

Simple
Quick energy
Little nutrient value
   Examples:
   Candy, syrup, etc.

Complex
Harder to digest
Long term energy
   Examples:
   Potatoes, Pasta, etc.

This makes for molecular tenacity, and it is with great reluctance that our bodies use the fat molecule for anything. So our bodies store it instead. This accumulation of fat occurs in vital passageways such as the twenty-two miles of our venous and arterial systems. Stored fat is dead weight that uglifies general appearance and hinders sport performances. Only during long-term aerobic activity (see chapter two) will the body liberate the fat molecules' energy.

Carbs

Carbohydrates. Carbon, hydrogen, oxygen. Carbs have excellent nutrient value and are found in foods such as pasta, bread, potatoes, rice, and fruits.

Every other week or so, a local Boulder, Colorado, restaurant features an all-you-can-eat pasta night for a $1.99 cover charge. On these nights, one may find athletes of all classes forking it in. Why? Their answers are similar: "I'm CARBING up!" Nutritionally, this victual extravaganza is logical. The pasta is nearly pure carbohydrate. For the athlete, this means energy. Carbs are broken down into basic sugars for use. Glycogen is the word used to identify this stored sugar form of body fuel.

I recommend a high-carb diet for athletes. We perform best under a high-carb dictatorship. Beware, though — the food industry is accelerating widespread use of "convenience" foods and ingredients. These highly processed substances contain an incredibly unsubstantiated surplus of sodium, sugar, and calories. Stay away. Stick to natural carbohydrates.

Protein

Protein foods contain the singular most important element that an athlete needs — amino acids. Aminos regulate our being. They keep our bodies in a "positive nitrogen balance" — a biologically favorable condition that insures cellular growth and repair. Without a consistent intake of high-quality amino acids, the athlete risks nitrogen loss and a corresponding stalemate of progress.

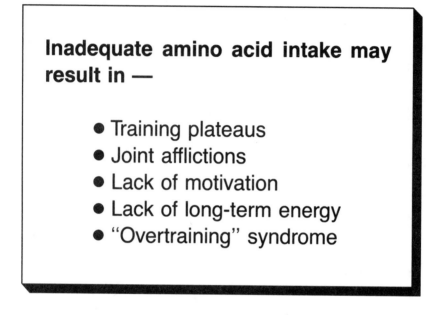

Inadequate amino acid intake may result in —

- Training plateaus
- Joint afflictions
- Lack of motivation
- Lack of long-term energy
- "Overtraining" syndrome

Some Functions of Amino Acids

- Facilitate cell and tissue growth.
- Promote oxygen utilization.
- Accelerate recovery from training.
- Improve immunological response.
- Reduce bodyfat levels via fatty acid utilization.
- Facilitate the manufacture of hormones and enzymes.

The bottom-line: In order to make and maintain outdoor athletic performance gains, two conditions must prevail:

1. The body must be in a positive nitrogen balance.

2. An intelligent, sport-specific, and progressive training stress must be repetitively applied with adequate recovery patterns.

A daily intake of amino acids — either through dietary protein foods or supplementation — will ensure that number one is met, and the use of this book's suggestions will take care of number two.

Vitamins and Minerals

Vitamins and minerals are specific compounds needed for cellular growth and other biochemical actions. Vitamins and minerals should be attained through a varied, natural diet. As insurance against the dietary mortification processes of the day, supplementing the diet with a vitamin/mineral packet may be in order. Vitamins and minerals work synergistically, that is, together. Taking vitamins and minerals separately is not as effective as absorbing them in unison.

Water

Here, the outdoor athlete must be most alert. The consequences of inadequate water intake are grim. Dehydration can occur in varying, but always detrimental, degrees.

I routinely will question a lagging athlete about his water intake. "Water?" echoes the increduous reply as though he has never heard of the substance. Amazingly, I notice this dehydrated attitude plaguing many athletes. Saturate an athlete with lots of water, and "chronic" injuries, inflammations, and training plateaus "mysteriously" vanish.

Water for the outdoor athlete is not merely a passive affair of input and output. Water is essential to the dynamic building and stabilization of cells. Water is the environmental interface between thousands of cellular components and is responsible for what H.T. Randall called the "... conversion and utilization of metabolizable nutrients and the excretion of ingested substances or their end-products of metabolism."

The Unbidden Sweet

The realm of performance-oriented nutrition is a sleek and demanding one. It is the most influential of the non-physical variables of total strength. Often we try to fool ourselves with fatuous justifications for a poorer, less attentive diet: "Well, I'm young, I don't need to pay attention to my diet," or, "Look at me, I'm lean, man! I can eat whatever I want, I won't get fat."

Learn this: THINK FROM THE INSIDE OUT. Just because one may appear lean, do not trust that the leanness is unconditional; congested arterial systems occur in marathon runners. Lazy-minded nutrition and tepid dietary discipline will take its toll in one way or another. Always the price will be paid.

Breeding the ability to resist unneeded but desired foods, though difficult, creates a deeper understanding and sense of self. It is this magnified discipline that bleeds into and affects our everyday life through subtle channels lying below conscious thought. It makes us stronger in ways many of us are not aware of.

Walk past the by-the-slices pizza parlors. Forego the cheesecake and choose the apple instead. The athletic must learn to cherish the healthful flow of nutrients, not calories, into the body. Operate efficiently on less quantity, but greater quality. As Horace noted, "The chief pleasure in eating does not consist in costly seasoning or exquisite flavor but in yourself." Bravo, bravo.

The athlete's diet is a disciplined one. Such a purifying process is diametrically opposed to the tides of fashionable society. It is the performing, aye, even the simply living, athlete who makes the statement of discipline. Whatever be the sport. By using dietary discipline as a tool, this statement rings clear and sharp. It is the internal self which orchestrates the external self. Food is fuel, nothing less, but nothing more. There is an old saying: "Appetite comes with eating." Be careful when, how, and what you eat.

Whole Foods

If nutrition has a point, it is biological balance, and in achieving that balance the key word is wholeness. Indeed, the scheme here might appear too simplistic, too Spartan to arouse anything more than dutiful curiosity. But go slow. I'll be the first person to tell you that the orientation toward balanced, regenerative, performance nutrition means much bleeding and healing of conditioned outlooks. I'll also be the last person to bend your arm convincing you to try something.

In Western eyes, pain, ache, and illness is considered "wrong" and something to be overcome. The forms vary: nerves are deadened, biochemicals and their actions are intercepted or substituted, or maybe something is removed. Defuse the awareness seems to be the operative command. John Gill's classic line comes to mind: "Ours is a society unwisely counseled by well-fed cardiologists, who are themselves plucked off the fairways with alarming regularity."

The Eastern approach lies nearer to athletic intuition. Here, health means nourishing the body so that it may heal and balance itself. It is by increasing — not attenuating — our concentration that the way to relieving and preventing imbalances is realized.

From the physiological perspective, whenever your body takes in an isolate (such as in processed foodstuffs), body molecules quickly attempt to reorganize it and transform this unusable isolate into a serviceable whole. Remember, Nature only recognizes wholeness. Feed your body something else and this haphazard cellular shuffling must occur. Addictive substances such as caffeine and alcohol have a twofold effect on this process. They intensify the helter-skelter and leave a potent wake of cellular destruction.

The athlete's task is to keep the cells clean. The purer the cellular membrane, the more efficiently the physiology operates. That thought makes good meditation when one considers that every minute 3 billion cells will die in each of us. How are you going about replacing them? Mere quantity alone is not enough. What about the quality of your replacement cells?

After a long struggle, I have found that living a regenerative, whole-food diet has proven incredibly successful for me and many of my athletes. My immunological responses seem in order — as I write these words, illness has prevented me from strength training only three times out of 2,184 workouts. I have yet to suffer any form of inflammation from my multi-sport intensities. If you wish specifics on the nutritional foods I work with, feel free to contact me.

Feeding the Psyche

"Hell is oneself,
Hell is alone, the other figures in it
merely projections. There is nothing to
escape from
And nothing to escape to. One is always
alone."

— *T.S. Eliot*

Motivation is the harnessing of one's emotions. I have always felt that motivation is an impulse directed toward achievement. The greater the value of the goal, the stronger the impulse to achieve it. Motivation incites fear and envy in those not in possession of it. Motivation divides the elite from the norm.

As a young nordic-combined skier in Durango, Colorado, I grew up on motivation. I challenged myself to its enduring call, daring my motivation to dwindle. Or to shatter. Long after teammates had showered and went off into the evening air toward family and food, I skied. For me, this was my home, my family. I cared little for the conventional comforts of the domestic sanctum. TV held as little attraction for me as did schoolwork; I spent little time with either. Instead, I skied — many times well into the night. I play-acted out my motivation on a cold and lonesome ski track. In the frost-lit darkness I came to know my skis not as simple staves of fiberglass and wood, but as living tools. I recall naming one "Pain," the other

I became a conduit of something much greater. *Photo courtesy Devon Daney.*

"Discipline." I drew energy from the snow beneath these tools and from the twilight swirling around my head. I learned to capture natural power. I became a conduit of something much, much greater.

There is tremendous beauty in motivation. And the magic of it all is that this natural outdoor athletic power works for everyone and in everyday situations and everyday goals and dreams. I recall a letter from a climber: "It's a beautiful feeling knowing how important goals are. Nothing is out of reach, all you need is a true heart. Live it up, life is the best!!" The words were written while my friend was in traction. He had broken his back three weeks prior.

There are no ordinary dreams for those who aspire to better themselves. The outdoor athlete is reminded of this during each venture.

Commitment to an effort is a hard thing for many to accept. It is easier to just climb or go skiing than to train for climbing and skiing. Then again, it is easier to eat the candy bar than to will one's self not to, or easier to get drunk and forget problems than to stand sober to their challenge. For those who have touched perfect joy through discipline there is no question of "easier or harder." For those who battle against mainstream mediocrity, a sagacious fulfillment of a different, deeper sort is realized. It is training that brought us here, to this bonfire of our growth. Motivation is the kindling. Constantly we must search for the kindling to keep the fire ablaze. To find it, we must dig around, stray from comfort to collect more, and sometimes break it off from larger things. More times than not, there's always some around. We just have to look closer.

This book challenges the outdoor lover to accommodate the master athlete within him. To lift weights, chase aerobic endeavors, nose-out good nutrition and live by its spark, to release in the periods of rest and recovery. To become attuned to the commitment

"Dedication to a goal that never wavers — resolution — This is the basic principle in the life of every truly great character. He who resolves upon any great and good end has, by that very resolution, clothed himself in power and has scaled the chief barrier to it." — Unknown

Commitment to an effort is a difficult thing for many to accept. Peter Hunt on Fire and Ice in Eldorado Canyon, Colorado.

of the athletic mindset and to mingle oneself within the presence of greatness. To reconstruct the latent faith in the being.

The Inner Outdoor Athlete

In his landmark book, *The Inner Game of Tennis*, a must for people of any athletic gender, W.T. Gallwey vividly brings forth an important truth for sports performance improvement. Gallwey shows two distinct selves — an operative ego, responsible for

A martial arts class in Santa Monica, California. This is an example of Kinesthetic Training done to promote postural and emotional balance. *Photo, Ilg archives.*

volitional decision-making processes, and a second self devoid of ego and which does not "think" but rather reacts and simply "does." It is this second self which the outdoor athlete has touched often. Training must be designed to accommodate this unthinking, instinctual character.

Training gives this inner self a chance to flee from the nerve center of our being and explode itself into actuality. Like the musical structure of Bach, we must begin from a seed and elaborate outward, focusing all at once on the Grand Scheme of Things. To do this, we first allow the thinking ego to relax. Beginning with the basics remains the athlete's saving respite. Indeed, going "backward" in technical ability is the key to moving forward in a more holistic and profound manner. This backward step is an expansion of self. Training accomplishes this like no other tool.

Below is a program contoured to such a philosophy. It is no over-simplification. It is designed to rectify misalignments of the

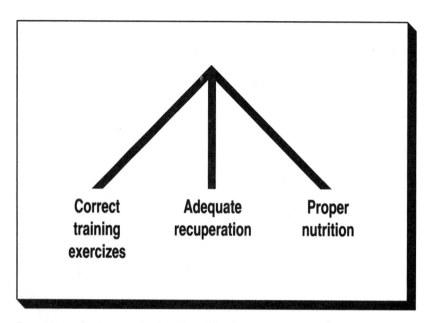

Correct	Adequate	Proper
training	recuperation	nutrition
exercizes		

Returning to basics remain the wise athlete's saving grace . . . innermost secrets reign within.

body/mind to produce a perfectly balanced whole. It recognizes the supreme importance of allowing the "being" to self-correct itself. The body teaches the mind.

This is basic stuff; do not, however, allow its brevity to ensnarl the ego. Innermost secrets hide amongst its manifestation. This program is preparatory play for the magic beyond. Train hard with it, but be watchful for and curb overt enthusiasm. There are none so righteous as the newly converted . . . initial ardor in any pursuit can override intelligence and invite damage.

In lieu of a qualified trainer, use discretion before beginning any training program. Contact a sports-knowledgeable physician; let him know of your training intent. Warm up well before strength training. For flexibility and exercise illustrations and reference, see Part II.

FIND YOUR LEVEL:

Level One = previous strength and CV training: 0-8 months of regular training.

Level Two = 8-12 months of both types of training.

Level Three = 1 year or more of both types of training done regularly

Train with the appropriate exercise prescription below for the amount of time indicated:

Level One = at least 3 months.

Level Two = at least 2 months.

Level Three = optional; recommended for 1 month.

After working out on the below program for the suggested time, one may then pursue the specific prescriptions contained in Part II. Don't rush the process; patience will be amply rewarded.

The Bountiful Basic Program

Note: In the following charts, the "x" symbolizes "times," as in: 3x8-10 (do three sets, eight to ten repetitions per set).

DAY ONE

— Strength Training —

Active warm-up, 10 minutes

Squats	3x10-12	Level 1; do Leg Press for first 2 weeks
Lunges	3x10-12	Levels 2 & 3
Leg Curls	4x10-12	
Calf Raises	4x12-15	(Vary foot positions)
Abdominal Crunches	3-4x20-30	Abdominals
Good Mornings	2x10	Lower back and thighs
Stair Running or Sprints	10x20 seconds	Levels 2 & 3 development; Levels 2 and 3 only: 80% effort

— CV Training —

Level 3 only = 30 minutes

DAY TWO

— Strength Training —

Pullups or Front Lat Pulldowns	3x8-10	Levels 2 & 3 do 4 sets
Dips	4x8-10	Use weight if needed
Seated Press	3x8-10	(Vary apparatus)
Lying Triceps Extensions	3x8-10	
Barbell Curls	3x8-10	Vary grip-width
Reach-Thru's	3x25 +/−	Levels 2 & 3 do "holding technique"

— CV Training —

None for all levels

DAY THREE

— Strength Training —

None for all levels

— CV Training —

Level One   30 minutes: low intensity, duration

Level Two   45-60 minutes: moderate intensity, duration

Level Three   60-? minutes, fartlek style

— Kinesthetic Training —

Pursue an "off sport" activity which enhances agility, balance, and/or temporal/motor skills. Examples of Kinesthetic Training activities might be ballet or gymnastic classes, a team sport, or a racquet sport. The thing is, I want your mind as well as your body reacting. This day, too, is a mandatory flexibility training day. This should be done in quiet solitude and last at least ten to fifteen minutes.

DAY FOUR

Start cycle over with DAY ONE.

Meditation Notes

Erase the Mind of Congestion
Stand Tall Inwardly and Out; Challenge Yourself
You Take Responsibility for Effort Intensity
Spine Erect, Breath Full and Deep, Yet Soft
Head Held High
Shoulder Girdle Dropped
Sensational Training Means Being Aware
Doing Exercise is One Thing; Being Exercised is Another
Study Yourself
Inner Calm; Outer Action
Nothing Really Matters But the Moment; Make It Count
"Ai Imawa" (Harmony Now)

Part II

Exercise Prescriptions and Illustrations

SPECIFICITY,
or the "SAID" PRINCIPLE

Specific adaptions to imposed demands

A training program must be
creatively centered upon which
adaptations are necessary or desirable

Specific strength tricks like the one-arm pullup are more conversational items
than valuable training movements . . . but they do look cool. *Photo by Mark Bogan.*

*"Man is so made, that whenever anything fires his soul
. . . impossibilities vanish."*

— LaFountaine

The process of acquiring fitness specific to one's sport needs is a challenging one. Recall the term, Periodzational Training. Periodzation means cycling one's training in order to elicit optimal performance while reducing the irritants of training. In many sports, periodzational techniques become quite complex. For the outdoor athlete, there is less call for intricacy; in most cases, the seasons help regulate the character of our training and performance.

Many of us, however, are multi-sport athletes, choosing to fill our year with a number of outdoor pursuits. Rick Sylvester, noted stunt man, skier, climber, and runner, points to this problematic "peak performance" endeavor: "It's hard to do each of them at a decent level, it affects the others . . . you're just trying to maintain all the time." Fortunately, many outdoor sports blend well with each other. The mountaineer who backcountry skis through winter will find the transition into an "in season" of mountaineering an easy one. In some outdoor sports, such as hang gliding, the value of periodzational training is debatable.

Bear in mind that periodzational training is for an athlete to PEAK for a certain time frame or performance. Seldom will users of this book wish to become so specialized; however, the philosophy is important, and I have interwoven their terms and concepts in the exercise prescriptions.

THE NEW POINTE SHOES   K. ROSSITER 1984

Examples of Periodzational Training

The Off-Season Phase

This is when the athlete "trains to train." It is sometimes called the "strength-building phase" or the "preparation phase." During this phase we identify major movement patterns and gear strength training sessions to emphasize an overall muscle and joint health balance and to maintain and/or improve cardiovascular fitness and endurance. This phase is also the time to INCREASE flexibility.

ABSTRACTS

Strength training involves multi-joint exercises and large muscle groups are given intense (4x6-10) workloads. The volume of CV training is discretionary to the sport, but it is usually varied to tax a number of physiological responses. Normally, most CV training done during this phase is of light to moderate volume and intensity. Flexibility is highly prioritized as is continuance of "off sport, conditioning activities."

First Transitional Phase

This phase seeks to adjust OFF-SEASON fitness gains to a more activity-specific training period. Flexibility remains highly prioritized. CV training is additionally emphasized.

ABSTRACTS

CV training is now placed on a higher attention level. Strength training switches character, including a more muscular endurance type of workload (3x15-20). Flexibility is pursued as a maintenance variable to allow more time for specific activity (s). Mental as well as conditioning skills constitute a heightened integral factor here.

In Season Phase

This phase maintains sport-specific strengths, flexibility, and CV fitness. It begins as specific activity is done regularly and lasts until said activity decreases.

ABSTRACTS

All training is considered secondary to specific activity. Strength training usually done in circuit style and aerobic/flexibility is done in moderate volumes.

Second Transition Phase

This is also known as the Active Rest Phase. This phase is overlooked and underestimated by many American athletes and coaches. This phase is undeniably important to the long-term progress and health of an athlete. This phase begins after consistent sport-specific activity lessens and is recommended for about one month before renewing this cyclic structure again with the OFF SEASON PHASE.

ABSTRACTS

This phase requires participation in recreational activities that will complement the movement patterns and motor skills of the outdoor athlete's primary sport pursuit. It is also a time to relax psychologically and physiologically from the demands of the athlete's main sport.

Movement

"Chiang said it time and again, 'Forget about faith! You didn't need faith to fly, you needed to understand flying . . . This is just the same!' "

— *Richard Bach,* Jonathan Livingston Seagull

In a strict sense, outdoor athletics are often a case of balance. Push and pull. Take rock climbing, for example. Reduced to elemental form we discover that the legs push, the arms and back pull. Forward (upward) movement is the result of overcoming a type of drag force (gravity).

There are certain lines of energy, lines of force to any movement. It is training done with concentration and elegance, that is the sincerest instructor of this teaching. One of the beautiful paradoxes to all training is that the most "advanced" training comes from the simplest truths resurfacing.

And so it is with every rep turned inward, every footfall turned under, every limb stretched a bit further, and each well-earned nutrient taken in, that we step that much closer to discovering another side to ourselves. It all starts here, get it!

There are certain lines of inner energy, an intangible avenue of force that governs all movement.

These principle training programs are your springboard into an elevated realm.

Principal Training Programs

The training programs that follow throughout the remainder of this book are offered to provide balance to your training. Their objective is harmony in preparation so that performance comes easier, more joyfully. Ultimately, they will widen the reader's receptivity to the inner, personal world of training. The energies and sensations are created by you, and therefore can only be realized in a dialogue you compose.

Break off on your own. NO ONE has the right to tell you what exercise program you HAVE to follow. Learn from my concepts — they are safe and very time/energy efficient — but create with an open mind. Tomorrow will never look the same.

All exercises and their descriptions can be found in Part III.

Composure Program

A program designed to reestablish the focus of training. This program is an ideal maintenance routine and is highly recommended after lay-offs.

I consider the world as made for me, not me for the world. It is my maxim therefore to enjoy it while I can, and let futurity shift for itself. — Tobias George Smollett

---

DAY ONE

— Strength Training —

Perform 3x8-10 for the first workout and 3x:30 seconds when this workout is repeated. Alternate between these two set-and-rep schemes for as long as this program is followed.

Exercise	Workout A	Workout B
Squats	yes	no
Touch n' Go Lunges	no	yes
Leg Curls Superset with: GP Squats	yes	yes
Pullups or Front Pulldowns	yes	no
Seated Rows	no	yes
Dips	yes	no
A L.C.M.	no	yes
Repetition Jerks	yes	no
Seated DB Press	no	yes
Lying Triceps Extension	yes	no
2-Bench Triceps	no	yes
Barbell Curls	yes	yes

Superset: Crunches &	no	yes
Stiff Leg Deadlifts		
3x20 of each.		
Superset: Reach-Thru's	yes	no
& Calf Raises		
3x20 of each		

DAY TWO

— Strength Training —

Recovery Day.

— Flexibility Training —

Thirty minutes minimum in a quiet room, full body.

— CV Training —

Begin:
1. 2 sets of Squat Jumps, 10-12 reps.
2. Sprinting:
   Set 1 = 2x100 yards at 70% effort. Recover fully.
   Set 2 = 4x50 yards at 70% effort. Recover fully.
3. 30-minute minimum of an aerobic (easy, steady effort) activity.

DAY THREE

Begin cycle over again with DAY ONE program.

Strength Program

Perform a warm-up/focus set with the empty bar. Then follow this repetition scheme to failure:

Set Number One:	12
Set Number Two:	6
Set Number Three:	3
Set Number Four:	3
Set Number Five:*	1

*Perform once every third workout.

Record all poundages closely. The following three powerlifts train the entire body. This is a day for increasing mental fortitude as well as physical perfection. Trust yourself, maintain good form, and uncork it! Recover fully between sets.

1. Squats   Alternate: A type of Leg Press

2. Bench Press   Alternate: Standing Press

3. Full Deadlift   Alternate: Top Deadlift

Composite Program

Rest as little as possible between sets. Perform each exercise for forty-five seconds to one minute, three sets. Learn to use and manipulate the resistance to "flirt" with muscular failure.

Discover pace, rhythm, and tempo. Be fluid. Find subtle energy pathways. Keep within the exercise.

1. Hang Cleans   Explosiveness; Breathing; Alternate: Seated or Bent Rowing

2. Pushups   Use knees if needed

3. Seated, Rotating   2 sets only
   DB Presses

4. Squats   Be as a piston; Breathing; Alternate: A type
                           of Leg Press

5. Leg Curls   Lying or Standing; Keep the "glutes;"
                           Alternate: Stiff Leg Deadlifts

6. Barbell Curls   Maintain strict form.
                           Alternate: Machines, DB's

7. 2-Bench Triceps   Drop one leg or add weight if needed

8. Calf Raises   Vary

9. Reach Thru's   See description for "holding" technique

10. Stiff Leg Deadlifts   30 seconds

This program contains many lessons in what I call "Muscle Economy." You will have to do this program a few times to discover what this means.

The "Get Lean" Prescription

"It is not enough to aim, you must hit."

— Unknown

To get lean, you will find yourself with a constant training partner — Diet. Acknowledging this, a friend of mine once wrote, "Urges do not matter. Action does." The bottom line on getting lean is to AVOID UNNEEDED CALORIE-DENSE FOODS.

Think hard about that one word — "Unneeded." How much food is really, honestly, "Needed"?

Once this is postulated, we must learn to accept food as a nutritional response to a biological need. Period. It is nothing more, but also nothing less; make a celebration of food intake! Earn this vital replenishment, and relish in its simplicity. Looking at food in this true perspective, we can then do away with our random indulgences.

Learn these few hints. They are vital:

High Fiber Foods: Low in calories, these foods offer a sensation of fullness due to a slow absorption process.

Processed Foods: Don't you dare. These "foods" are commercially designed to go down rapidly and make you want more.

Moderate Meat Intake: Biology shows us that a human's convoluted digestive tract is far more suitable for slower moving fiber foodstuffs than the quick-to-decompose meaty foods.

Eat Slowly: This offers intrinsic appetite control mechanisms an opportunity to function.

Appetite Comes with Eating: Do not overdramatize foods.

Exercise: Some of this program's benefits: stimulation of body-fat-metabolizing enzymes; muscle cells increase, requiring more energy to subsist; psychological effects discourage severe dieting which has been shown to destroy fat-burning enzymes.

For each pound of fat we lose, we increase our available oxygen one percent or more.

Get Lean Exercise Prescription, 5-Day Cycle

DAY ONE

— Strength Training —

Active warm-up = 10 minutes

	Workout A	Workout B
Leg Press Superset with Back Squats	3x15 of each	None
Barbell Hacke Squats Superset with Touch n' Go Lunges	None	3x10-12 of each
Leg Curls Superset with GP Squats	3x15 of each	Same as Workout A
Calf Work (Vary apparatus)	5x15x30	3x8-10

— CV Training —

Pick a form of aerobic training and perform thirty minutes of moderate intensity.

DAY TWO

— Strength Training —

Upper body

Active warm-up

Seated Rows Superset with a Lateral Chest Movement (L.C.M.)	3x8-10 of each	None
Tri-Set:		
1. Front Lat Pulldowns	None	8-10
2. Bench Press (vary)	None	8-10
3. Rotating DB Press	None	10-12
2-Bench Triceps Superset with Barbell Curls	3x15/8-10	None
Lying Tricep Extensions	None	3x8-10
Alt. DB Curls	None	3x8-10
Barbell Curls	3x12-15	None
Abdominal Work (vary)	about 5-8 minutes	
Warm-Down	10-30 minutes	

— CV Training —

None. Perform fifteen to thirty minutes of Flexibility Training.

DAY THREE

— Strength Training —

None

— CV Training —

Perform sixty minutes minimum of good intensity.

DAY FOUR

— Strength Training —

Do COMPOSITE PROGRAM

— CV Training —

Thirty minutes of interval-style training. Be creative.
See Day Two of Composure Program.

DAY FIVE

— Strength Training —

None

— CV Training —

Forty-five minutes minimum. Good intensity; do not perform the same activity as you did on Day Three. Also, perform at least fifteen minutes of Flexibility Training.

Training Abstracts

Some things to remember while training:

AN ACTIVE WARM-UP

This session of heart-rate elevating action has physiological and psychological aspects which are critical for a healthy and productive workout. These initial moments can be viewed as a joyful release from stagnant life. It serves as a time to tune into the warmth of the body. The active warm-up needs to be but several minutes, but the benefits are immense. Though the full spectrum of the active warm-up still needs some technical exploration, contemplate these events while your circulation begins to flow:

- Increased tissue temperature results in a lower incidence of musculoskeletal injuries.

- Joint range of motion is improved due to the connective tissue growing more elastic.

- A smoother cardiovascular response transpires.

- Muscle contraction and transmission of kinesthetic signals is enhanced.

FLEXIBILITY

This is vital for overall joint health and longevity. Flexibility is achieved by progressive stretching sessions and techniques. Flexibility training should be done in a relaxed, mind-calming manner with an environmental emphasis on quietude. I don't ask much, about two to three times per week for fifteen to thirty minutes or so. Flexibility is a beautiful place to be; it is well worth the drive for anyone. Helpful books are *Stretching* by Bob Anderson and *Staying Supple* by John Jerome.

NUTRITION

An athlete's twenty-four-hour training partner:

- Take in a consistent amount of high-quality amino acids. I recommend Amino 1000 by Uni-Pro (1-800-621-6070).

- Regular intake of vitamins, minerals, and other base level nutrients such as anti-oxidants is a sound philosophy. Research.

- Eat simply. Meals should be a response to exercise. Learn to ignore random urges. Here is the key: A lot of complex carbohydrates, moderate, consistent protein (amino acid) intake, and very little fat. (See Nutrition, page 48)

ATHLETIC TECHNIQUE AND MOTIVATION

Train in good tempo. Tap into the flow of your inner rhythm, it is always there. Train elegantly but with powerful and precise control. Make each training session worthwhile. This can be done many ways. Love your exercise, it is yours. Only you hold the simultaneous miracle of creating and discovering your unlimited potential. Most of all, do not forget the lessons of your training. Take your workout with you wherever you go and use it in whatever you do.

I will say it again. Most of all, do not forget the lessons of your training. Take your workout with you, everywhere, and remember, a final realization for any athlete: *"Things Take Time."*

Surfaces of a more meaningful life rise to itch at us deeply. A woman climber high on Annapurna. *Photo courtesy of Sue Giller.*

Specific Training Prescriptions

General Mountaineering and Advanced Backpacking

> *"I will exchange a city for a sunset,*
> *the tramp of legions for a winds*
> *wild cry,   and all the*
> *braggard thrusts of steel triumphant*
> *for one far summit, blue against the sky."*
>
> — *Marie Blake*

When given a chance, a caged animal will bolt from its stall. In those initial moments of delicious freedom the head tosses to and fro, legs kick high, and a tail may whip at sweet, grassy air. Smiles are etched upon the faces of onlookers, sighs a silent soundtrack to the animals frolicking.

Mountaineering offers the opportunity for us to bolt from our stall. For many of us, it is this spilling of our inner selves onto the glacial terrain and into the mountain air that is essential. Self-importance hesitates while in rocky and snow-strewn heights giving way to a more miraculous wonder. Surfaces of a more meaningful life rise to itch at us deeply. And, if you're like me, we will gladly return time and again to scratch at it. Whatever be the cost.

MAJOR MOVEMENT PATTERNS

A mountaineer's kinesiological parameters are similar to those of the backpacker or hiker. The major differences are physiological and can be recognized primarily by a two-fold effect:

1. The INTENSITY of stressed musculature and strengths, and

2. The direct upper limb involvement for technical movements.

COMMON INJURY SITES

The breathing body.
Mountaineering and advanced backpacking are dangerous sports. A disgruntled nine-to-five executive may talk himself (forgive the masculine pronoun) into thinking that he is ready for any wilderness adventure, yet rarely will he consider his physical status. The mind may be ready for the south face of Dhalagriri, but the body is in the walk-through-the-park mediocrity. Irresponsibility in preparing for the mountains has a tendency to breathe living irony into the saying, "There are no victims, only volunteers."
Endurance.
There is little question to the value of endurance to both mountaineers and backpackers. Endurance alludes to the potential of one's body to supply a consistent amount of emergy to the working musculature. We need to circumvent fatigue as much as possible while simultaneously achieving maximum efficiency for long and strenuous journeys. CV training is instrumental in developing and enhancing endurance capabilities.

Perhaps most beneficial to the properly trained mountaineer is the development of SLOW, OXIDATIVE muscle fiber types. These fibers are "SLOW to contract, but RESISTANT to fatigue." They possess a highly developed oxidative system, enabling them to sustain moderate workloads over a long period of time.

Strength.

What does a mountaineer or backpacker DO that requires strength? Sport scientists list numerous different components of strength. They range from biochemical qualifiers to neurological considerations, to even psychosocial factors. Perhaps most interesting is the muscle-fiber composition dimension. The following training programs enrich many of these factors.

My advice: Go to the mountain with as much strength as possible, for the heights will soon swindle most of it.

Some functional examples of strength valuable in the technical mountains is hauling and overall rope work. Efficient strength is tantamount to a strong team. I've had instances when non-strength trained partners, subservients to failing strength, have had to rely disproportionately upon me. Strength-training is not only a responsibility to yourself, it is also a moral responsibility to your colleagues.

Another type of strength is required for the backpacker and mountaineer. I call it STABILIZATION STRENGTH. Intra-muscular tension is constant for any pack-bearing animal. An everlasting isometric contraction is continually needed to stabilize one's pack. The properly strength-trained outdoor athlete, accustomed to weight-bearing stresses, retards intra-muscular fatigue. Additionally, ligamentous strain is much less likely for the strength-trained athlete than the soft and woundable joint tissue connecting the non-strengthened athlete.

I remember a student's realization as I coached her through a first encounter with Back Squats — a deep knee bend with weight. In short order, a light of understanding lit the area where we stood. She felt the deep, forceful contractions taking up residency in the powerful muscles of her "Power Chain" musculature, the hips and legs. It was only a couple of days later that she excitedly related how the manifestation of the weight-training exercise was taking effect on her mountain excursions.

To restate the point here, the mountaineer should seek strength through the manner of tension. For example, the muscles of the abdominal wall and lower back should possess high, not only stabilization strength, but also explosive strength in order to fully realize the efforts of the lower and upper body.

CONSIDERATIONS FOR THE
HIGH-ALTITUDE MOUNTAINEER

A number of illnesses are derived from the lofty heavens of high altitude. Mountain sickness is a common example. One's oxidative system usually is the stage upon which these afflictions perform. The reason this is so is because our oxidative or aerobic system involves the maintenance and utilization of oxygen — a misty ingredient at high altitudes. The body, sensing this deprivation of a vital substance, begins perfunctory survival tasks to compensate for this environmental change. Such self-preserving techniques are symptomatically felt in any number of ways. Irregular breathing has been experienced by many mid-altitude trekkers. This common condition can be noticed in one's relatives from the flat lands as they come "up" and into the mountains. As long as this accelerated breathing is not escorted by other mountain sickness symptoms, do not be worried.

In cognizance of the fact that this is a book on strength training, I feel an indirect responsibility to provide awareness in regard to the strength of knowledge. Each mountaineer and backpacker should become familiar with the techniques for graded ascents. I now refer you to some excellently written and well-researched material indited by Peter Hackett, M.D. His book, *Mountain Sickness*, should be vested in the backpack side pockets of anyone hoofing any path of any incline. I trust the responsibility of detailed research in the following subject matter to the reader.

GRADED ASCENT

Reprinted by personal permission: Mountain Sickness: Prevention, Recognition, Treatment, *by Peter Hackett, M.D. (American Alpine Club, Inc.).*

In those individuals susceptible to acute mountain sickness, the faster the rate of ascent, the more likely they are to develop symptoms. Prior to altitude exposure, one presently has no way of knowing or predicting performance at altitude. Those who do well at altitude will most likely do well again, given the same rate of ascent. Those with repeated exposures seem to do better each time, in fact. However, throwing all caution to the wind, and steaming up to altitude will often make one realize his "AMS threshold." Then again, differences in hydration, exertion, diet, etc., may alter one's susceptibility to acute mountain sickness on any given exposure. For newcomers to altitude we recommend:

- Do not fly or drive to altitude. Start below 3,000 meters and walk up.

- If taken passively to altitude, do not exert yourself or move higher for the first twenty-four hours.

- Once above 3,000 meters, limit your net gain in altitude (your sleep altitude) to 300 meters per day (1,000 feet).

- Carry high and sleep low. It is best to go a little higher than the sleeping altitude, and then descend, instead of sleeping at the maximum altitude reached that day. Camp in valleys, for example, instead of high ridges between valleys, while you are acclimatizing.

- Take an "acclimatization" night for every 1,000 meters gain in elevation, starting at 3,000 meters or so. (Thus, every three days while still ascending.) This means sleeping at altitude for two consecutive nights. The day can be spent relaxing or hiking up a ridge, bouldering, or whatever, depending on how you are feeling. People with symptoms of acute mountain sickness should rest.

Even those with considerable altitude experience are advised to follow these recommendations to derive maximum benefit of acclimatization. It may mean the difference between a marginally enjoyable struggle and a comfortable, thoroughly enjoyable (and safe) trip. Why suffer?

OFF-SEASON PROGRAMS: SPLIT ROUTINE METHOD (MOUNTAINEERING)

DAY ONE

— Strength Training —

Lower body.

Workout A	Workout B
Back Squats	Jump Squats with GP Squats (30 seconds of each)
Barbell Hacke Squats	Narrow Stance Leg Press (vary)
"Touch 'n Go" Lunges	Leg Extensions, last set descending
Leg Curls Superset with Stiff Leg Deadlifts	Leg Curls (Ilg variant)
Seated Calf Raises	Standing Calf Raises (3-way)
Russian Twists	Concentration Crunches
Abdominal Wheel (3x10-20)	Leg Raises (vary)

— CV Training —

Thirty minutes.

— Flexibility Training —

Ten minutes minimum.

— Strength Training —

Perform 4x8-10 of each exercise except where noted. Rest period should not exceed one minute. Performance of each set should be done to momentary muscular failure. Alternate workout sessions from A to B.

DAY TWO

— Strength Training —

Upper body: Perform 4x8-10 of each exercise except where noted. Rest approximately 45 seconds between each set.

Workout A	**Workout B**
Pullups (a feeble pullup alternative is the front lat pulldown)	V-Handle Pulldowns
Hang Cleans	2-way "Ilgs"
Dips	Bench Press (vary bench angle)
Bent-Arm Pullovers (2x10-12)	Machine or DB Flyes (vary angle)
Seated Press	Seated Press behind Neck (2 sets only) Side Lateral Raises (2 sets only)
2 Bench Triceps (assisted negatives if possible)	Lying Tricep Extensions (2 sets only)

Barbell Curls   Alt. DB Curls (2 sets only)
                                 Machine Curls (2 sets only)

Wrist Curl Superset with
Reverse Wrist Curls
Do 10-12x20-25

— CV Training —

Twenty minutes, low intensity.

— Flexibility Training —

Discretionary.

DAY THREE

— Strength Training —

None.

— Kinesthetic Training and/or CV Training —

Thirty to sixty minutes of each, your choice of CV activity.

— Flexibility/Mind Training —

Thirty to ? minutes in a quiet atmosphere.

END OF CYCLE.

OFF-SEASON PROGRAMS: FULL-BODY WORKOUT ALTERNATIVE (MOUNTAINEERING)

This program should be done three times per week on non-consecutive days. Alternate workouts from Workout A to Workout B.

Exercise	Workout A	Workout B
Squats	3x10-12	None
Narrow Stance Leg Press	None	4x15-20 quick tempo
"Touch 'n Go" Lunges	3x12-15	None
Barbell Hacke Squats	None	3x12-15
Leg Curls	3x8-10	3x12-15
Pullups	4x8-10	4x BW
Hang Cleans	4x8-10	None
Seated Rows (vary)	None	3x10-12
Dips	4x8-10	4x BW
Flyes (vary)	None	3x10-12
Bench Press (vary)	3x8-10	None
Seated Press	None	3x10-12
Side Lateral Raises	3x10-12	None
Pressdowns	3x8-10	Superset with Curls

Barbell Curls	3x8-10	Superset with Pressdowns (3x12-15)
Reach Thru's	3x20-25	None
Stiff Leg Deadlifts	3x10-15	None
Russian Twists	None	3x20
Seated Good Mornings	None	3x10-12
Calf Raises or Presses	3x10-12	3x30-50

FIRST TRANSITIONAL PHASE: FIVE-DAY CYCLE (MOUNTAINEERING)

DAY ONE

— Strength Training —

Lower body, see below.

— CV Training —

Interval work consisting of three to ten sets of two to three minutes of high-intensity work.

— Flexibility Training —

20 minutes, post workout.

— Strength Training —

Perform three sets ot twelve to fifteen reps each. ☆ indicates this exercise should be supersetted with the exercise which follows it. Limit rest to forty-five seconds between each completed super-set, while striving for as little rest as possible within the superset:

Exercise:

Jump Squats ☆
GP Squats

Vertical or Diagonal Leg Press ☆
Touch 'n Go Lunges

Barbell Squats or Barbell Hackes ☆
Leg Extensions

Leg Curls ☆
Stiff Leg Deadlifts

Standing Calf Raises ☆
Donkey Calf Raises

DAY TWO

— Strength Training —

Upper body; see below.

— CV Training —

Low-intensity, moderate volume.

— Flexibility Training —

Ten minutes, minimum.

— Strength Training —

Perform three sets of twelve to fifteen repetitions of each exercise, concentrating on rhythm and form. ☆ indicates a superset with the exercise which follows it. Recovery philosophy is the same as in DAY ONE.

Hang Cleans ☆
Dips or Pushups

Repetition Jerks

Barbell or Decline Curls ☆
2-Bench Triceps or Pressdowns

Hanging/Suspended Leg Raises ☆
Twist Crunches

DAY THREE

Recovery day from strength training. Do a high-volume/high-intensity. CV training session of your choice. Flexibility Training: thirty minutes. Kinesthetic Training suggested.

DAY FOUR

— Strength Training —

Follow COMPOSITE PROGRAM.

DAY FIVE

— Strength Training —

Recovery day.

— CV Training —

Stair running or uphill sprints = 5 ? sets of two-minute high-intensity work periods followed by a full recovery period.

I am going in search of a great perhaps. Francois Rabelais climber; Mark Sylvestri.

Technical Climbing Programs

As a few of you know, and others may have guessed, technical climbing is, and has been for over a decade, my sincerest and most beautiful athletic acquaintance. I will not try to fool you or waste reading time: Technical climbing transcends commonplace athletic endeavor. It always has, and hopefully, should we chase our star kindly, always will. It is the singular sport with which I have been involved that I know changes the way its participants view life.

For all its depth and ability to exaggerate one's emotional complexity, climbing retains a soft underbelly of simplicity. It is the one variable in its multifactorial being that girders James Ramsey Ullman's "refreshment of the spirit." It is this paradox that breathes communicative life into the sport.

Perhaps it is this outright implausibility to our activity that makes it the most important to proper preparation.

COMMON INJURY SITES

Elbows. Tendonitis. More aptly: Bilateral tendonitis specific unto the medial epicondyle. I'm sick of hearing about it. I'm weary of treating it. Borne from improper (imbalanced) strength-training done too specifically.

MAJOR MOVEMENT PATTERNS

Documented literature on the biomechanics of technical climbing are nonexistent. In the most sterile vantage, climbing is another case of push and pull; the arms and back pull, the legs propel or push. Forward (upward) movement is the result of overcoming a drag force called gravity, by propulsion upwards.

Arm Movement: For clarity's sake, a model of a climber performing "face climbing" moves is used. Upon the pulling phase, horizontal abduction and inward rotation of the gleno-humeral joint is made. Primary emphasis occurs deep within the latissimus dorsi and teres complex. The biceps brachii assist this action. Upper torso alignment is centered by isometric contraction of the abdominal and lumbar muscles.

Leg Movement: Foot position is, of course, ever-changing. As initiation of climbing normally mandates bringing the legs up to a level even with the trunk, the gluteals, and illipsoas, are necessary for this work. Weighting the leg is done by leg extension and is the responsibility of the quadriceps. Strong endurance qualities must be present in the calf musculature; the gastrocnemius and the soleus.

OFF-SEASON:3-DAY SPLIT ROUTINE (TECHNICAL CLIMBING)

DAY ONE

— Strength Training —

Limit rest between sets to forty-five seconds.

Ilg "prop work" training on a pegboard. *Photo by Mark Bogan.*

Exercise	**Workout A**	**Workout B**

[Before pullups, if possible, do some "Prop Work," i.e., crack machines, pegboard, practice one-arms, etc. See illustration.]

Pullups	4x BW	3x6-8
Front Lat Pulldowns	None	3x8-10 "lsd"

Hang Cleans	None	3x10-12
2-Way Ilgs or Seated Rows	3x8-10	None
Dips	4x BW	4x6-8 "lsba"
Dumbbell Flyes	3x10-12	None
Bench Press	None	3x10-12
Seated Press (vary)	3x10-12	3x10-12
Lying Triceps Extension	4x10-12	None
Pressdowns	None	3x10-12
Barbell Curls	4x8-10	None
Seated Alt. DB Curls	None	4x8-10 "lsd"
Reach Thru's	4x20-35	None
Abdominal Wheel	None	3x1:00
Hanging Leg Raises	3x1:00	None
Inversion Situps	None	3-4x20

— CV Training —

None.

— Flexibility Training —

Ten to thirty minutes.

DAY TWO

— Strength Training —

Exercise	Workout A	Workout B
Squats	4x8-10	None
Superset (3X): Leg Press with	None	15-20
Lunges (vary)	None	10-12
Jump Squats	3x30 seconds	See Workout A
Ski Stance	3x1:00	None
Superset:		
(1) GP Squats with	None	3x1:00
(2) Leg Curls (vary)	3x8-10	3x12-15
Calf Raises (vary)	4x8-10	4x2:00

— CV Training —

Twenty minutes minimum, type is discretionary.

DAY THREE

— Strength Training —

None.

— Kinesthetic Training —

One to two hours, train creatively. Examples: Buildering, bouldering, wire walking, ballet, gymnastics, etc. If possible, go climbing.

— Flexibility Training —

Fifteen minutes minimum. Quiet atmosphere.

— CV Training —

Type: Fat-burning day. Your choice. Duration: Forty-five to sixty minutes minimum, low-intensity.

METHODOLOGY NOTES: On day four, begin cycle over at DAY ONE. Once per month perform a "strength program."

TRANSITIONAL PHASE PROGRAM (TECHNICAL CLIMBING)

Monday and Thursday	Monday	Thursday
"Prop Work"	10 minutes	
Pullups	4x6-8	4x BW
Dips	4x6-8	4x BW
Bent Over Rows	4x8-10	3x12-15
Bench Press or DB Flyes	4x8-10	3x12-15
Press Behind Neck	3x10-12	3x1:00
Tricep Extensions	4x8-10	4x1:00
Barbell Curl	4x8-10	4x1:00
Tricep Pressdowns	3x10-12	3x1:00
Alt. DB Curls	3x10-12	3x1:00
Reverse Wrist Curls	4x25-30	4x25-30

Tuesday and Friday	Tuesday	Friday
Superset (3x): Squat Jumps with GP Squats	30 seconds 30 seconds	None None
Squats	5x15-30	3x10-12
Lunges (vary)	3x10-12	3x10-12
Leg Curls	5x15-30	3x10-12

Calf Raises (vary)	4x8-10	5x1:00
Hanging Leg Circulars	4x?	4x?
Reach Thru's	4x25	4x25
Leg Raises	3x1:00	3x1:00

Wednesday

Buildering, bouldering, or creative off-specific activity. CV Training should be thirty minutes minimum, low to moderate intensity. Include some sprints.

Saturday and Sunday

Climb. If no climbing can be done, insert a COMPOSITE PROGRAM (one day only) with some off-specific activity and/or some specific activity.

TRANSITIONAL PHASE PROGRAM: FULL-BODY PRESCRIPTION (TECHNICAL CLIMBING)

Methodology Notes: Alternate the following program on non-consecutive days with the COMPOSITE PROGRAM. Below, rest between sets should be thirty seconds. All sets to MMF. STRENGTH PROGRAM once per month.

Squats or Leg Press	4x12-15
Leg Curls	3x8-10
Pullups	3x BW (use props)
Hang Cleans	4x12-15
Dips	4x BW
Seated Press (vary)	3x12-15
Lying Triceps Extension	4x10-12
Curls (vary)	4x10-12
Standing Calf Raises	5 x 5 x 30 x 30
Stiff Leg Deadlifts	3x12-15
Abdominal Work (vary)	High-Volume, High-Intensity

On off days from strength training, perform a minimum of forty-five minutes of CV work of moderate intensity. Flexibility Training should be done for twenty minutes minimum. Pay strict attention to caloric intake. Think lean.

ON-SEASON TRAINING (TECHNICAL CLIMBING)

Perform the following exercises in circuit style (moving from one exercise to another with little, if any, rest between the respective exercises). Reach Momentary Muscular Failure between fifteen to twenty repetitions unless otherwise indicated. This program can be done one, two, or three times per week. Make certain that multiple training sessions occur on non-consecutive days.

Start: Circuit One =

(1) Pullups (with props if possible) or Front Lat Pulldowns

(2) Dips

(3) Crunches, 25 reps

(4) Squats, 10 to 12 reps

(5) Leg Curls

Stop, rest for 1:00. Do this circuit two to three more times.

Start: Circuit Two =

(6) Leg Raises, 35 reps

(7) Dumbbell Seated Press or Walk on Hands

(8) Barbell Curls

(9) Pressdowns

(10) Calf Raises (vary), 15 to 20 reps

(11) Stiff Leg Deadlifts

Stop. Rest, begin again at Number 6. Do this three times.

— CV Training —

Your choice, moderate intensity consisting of thirty- to sixty-minute sessions done two to three times per week. Include some sprinting (5x 50 yards or equivalent fartlek technique) during these sessions.

A FOOTNOTE ON FINGERS

Increased muscle force that pulls repetitively upon a joint is met by an increase in tendon/ligament strength. The holistic strength training described throughout this book develops a stronger muscle to connective tissue relationship, whereas hanging on small edges and holds does not. Improper integration of fingerboard training is an example. Here the athlete hangs at arms length while "working" the board. By doing so most of the tension (electricity) is removed from the musculature and transferred directly to the skeletal system. Without a warm and working musculature to distribute this tension, an excessive amount is continuously placed upon vulnerable finger-joint tissue. Overuse symptoms will occur in response to such "training." Cases of inflamed tissue from ill-prepared designs appear as quickly as one week and as slowly as many years. The following program has been used extensively by many previously injured climbers and other athletes with superb and progressive results. It can be followed throughout the year.

Off-Season Phase: Include this circuit once every three to four days:
(1) Wrist Curls   :30
(2) Reverse Wrist Curls: :30
(3) Recover: :30
Repeat for three to four circuits.

Transition/Pre-Season Phase: Same frequency and volume as above.
(1) Wrist Curls   1:00
(2) Reverse Wrist Curls   :30
(3) Finger Curls   :30
(4) Recover   :30 — no rest

On-Season Phase: Weekend Athletes — Repeat above program or perform bouldering. Seasoned Athletes — Once per week perform above program, then go bouldering at a moderate intensity for thirty to sixty minutes.

ON-SEASON: BODYWEIGHT ONLY PROGRAM (TECHNICAL CLIMBING)

Perform up to three times a week on non-consecutive days. Perform circuit style. Do circuit three times with a three-minute rest between circuits. All sets to MMF.

(1) Rope Climb or Pegboard (go up and down till momentary failure)

(2) Pullups

(3) Pushups

(4) Jump Squats, 30 seconds only

(5) "Holding" Reach Thru's

(6) Dips

(7) Two Bench Triceps

(8) Undergrip Pullups

Stop, rest, go again.

On off days from strength training, perform low-intensity/moderate- to high-volume CV activity and a flexibility training session of twenty minutes minimum.

SOME THOUGHTS AND REASSURANCES . . .

Many climbers I've talked with express apprehension regarding maintenance of strength levels while on trips. Do not grow anxious about strength levels. One can expect absolute strength levels to increase from 1 to 3 percent per seven days of training (at first strength comes faster due to neural adaptations, but soon that improvement will slow). You can expect to lose such gains at about the same rate. Good nutrition and a high activity level appear to retard this process. Once a strengthbase has been established (say after a consistent OFF-SEASON effort), that foundation remains resilient. Do not let the lack of training interfere with your psyche while on trips and forced lay-offs. Be creative and stay as active as possible.

NOTE TO SPECIALISTS

The above program designs allow complete transfer strengths into the specialized sports of technical ice climbing and bouldering. The ice climber may wish to keep an open and creative mind to the "Prop Work" suggestions listed above. Two towels draped over a pullup bar and grasped in either hand, then doing pullups and "static holds" from them, is an excellent example of sport-specific ice-climbing training that can be injected into the above programs.

Boulder specialists have a more definite need for "dynamic power" in their training. Exercises such as Powercleans, Hang Cleans, and Power Pullups are instrumental in maximizing this type of fast-twitch power.

I've been pleasantly surprised by the number of requests for specific training from spelunkers. Beyond base-level physical preparation, I suggest the spelunker prepare for his sport using the technical rock climbing prescriptions outlined in this book. As a note, one caver writes that performing both athletic and everyday activities "in darkness or with both eyes closed . . . helps my sensitivity in caves."

Again, in the gym we train primarily for "principal" strength, allowing the sport itself to develop the "specific" strengths.

Backcountry Skiing Programs

". . . Yet having known, life will not press so close,
And always I shall feel time ravel thin about
me.
For once I stood in the white, windy presence
of eternity.

— E. Tjetjens

Sixten Jernber, the legendary Swedish cross-country ski racer, was asked what could be done technique-wise if one's skis weren't performing well due to waxing problems. Sixten replied monotonely, "Just ski a bit harder."

The work profile of the backcountry skier is extensive. For the most part, backcountry skiing is largely an aerobic activity of low-intensity/high-duration effort. However, there are times when the terrain, altitude, snow, and environmental conditions can turn this moderate affair into a huffing, puffing, wheezing, and thrashing anaerobic onslaught. Proper conditioning keeps the enjoyment in and the frustration out.

MOVEMENT PATTERNS

The basic motion of the backcountry skier is much different than that of today's "track" skier. The "V"-skate technique has completely altered the character of competitive cross-country skiing. In the back country, however, no man-made icy highway is paved for the purist. In these lush meadows of powder-filled fun, the classic diagonal stride or perhaps more aptly put as the diagonal shuffle, remains the only practical technique.

The primary movement pattern occurs at the hip joint. This articulation allows freedom of movement along many axes relative to that joint. The movements to be trained at the hip joint are extension, flexion, hyperextension, and a bit of abduction and adduction.

Backcountry skiing: Re-defining the essentials of life. *Photo by Richard DuMais.*

Upper body strength is crucial to the action of backcountry skiing. Besides acting as counterlevers to momentum created by lower body limb movement, arms driven by back musculature must support and propel one's body in a forward plane. This action is greatly exaggerated on uphill terrain. The upper arms are elemental to this movement, yet realistically, this arm action is really a by-product of the back musculature. Training with this fact in mind will yield significantly positive results.

The lower back muscles are critical to the skier. These muscles must remain isometrically contracted for the duration of one's skiing. These muscles support and assist the functioning of more superficial muscles. Poor technique is sometimes the source of post skiing lower back pain, but more often we can assume the skier has not properly strength trained the area. Recall that with a proper strength-training program comes more flexibility and more efficient toxin removal. Doesn't that sound better than dealing with chronic back pain? Backpacks create greater stress due to changes in postural angles. Stabilization of mechanically efficient body position, therefore, must be accomplished via the strength of this midsection.

DELINEATION OF PERFORMANCE OBJECTIVES

It is critical to cycle one's training so that the greatest training effect occurs as ski season begins. Adequate snowfall often signals the start of the long-awaited ON-SEASON. Thus, a clear line is drawn for a periodzational training philosophy.

COMMON INJURY SITES

Although backcountry skiing is an ideal workout, one that is very taxing, yet giving on the joints, injuries do occur. According to my research, among skiers who incurred injuries while skiing, most said that lower back pain was the greatest problem. Consequently, preventive training emphasis should be targeted to this area.

TECHNIQUE TRAINING

By keeping the neuromuscular pathways fresh during the OFF SEASON, the transition onto snow will be easier. Several dry-land training methodologies exist for the out-of-snow skier. (Refer to Chapter 2 for devices aiding the off-season skier.)

"THE THUNDER FLY" OFF-SEASON PROGRAM (BACKCOUNTRY SKIING)

Duration: Three to four months

Frequency: Three-day cycle

Abstracts: Every third cycle, perform a STRENGTH PROGRAM day

DAY ONE

— Strength Training —

Exercise	Workout A	Workout B
Active Warm-Up		
Split Jumps	3x10-12	None
Squat Jumps	None	3x10-12
Back Squats	3x8-10	None
Front or Hacke Squats	None	3x12-15

Touch 'n Go Lunges Superset with Stiff Leg Deadlifts	Perform on both workouts, 3x10-12 of each	
Leg Curls with Ilg variant	4x10-12	4x8-10 "lsd"
Calf Work (vary)	4x10-12	4x8-10 "lsd"

— CV Training —

Perform three - ? sets of one of the following:

(1) Hill bounding with poles

(2) Stair sprints

(3) Uphill springs

(4) Aerobic device training

Each set needs to have a work/recovery ratio of 1:00/1:00 with the work phase being of high intensity (effort).

DAY TWO

— Strength Training —

Active Warm-Up

Power Cleans	3x8-10	None
Hang Cleans	2x10-12	None
Pullups or Front Lat Pulldowns	None	4x up to 12
Dips	3x8-10	None
Bench Press	None	5x15x30
Seated Press (vary)	3x8-10	None
Repetition Jerks	None	3x12-15
Curls (vary)	3x6-8	3x12-15 "lsd"
DB Kickbacks	2x15-20	2x15-20
Lying Triceps Extension	3x6-8	None
Pressdowns	None	2x8-10
2 Bench Triceps	None	2x25
Seated Twisting	Perform on both workouts; 3x1:00 with 1:00 recovery	

Abdominal work (vary exercises, intensity, and volume)

Optional: Superset: Reverse wrist curls (twenty reps) with wrist curls (six to eight reps) for three sets.

— CV Training —

None.

DAY THREE

— Strength Training —

None.

— CV Training —

Perform long duration (no less than thirty minutes), low-intensity aerobic training of your choice. Also, Flexibility Training; full body, no less than thirty minutes in a quiet atmosphere.

THE "THUNDER FLY" OFF-SEASON TWO-DAY CYCLE VARIATION (BACKCOUNTRY SKIING)

DAY ONE

Full-body strength-training day.

No CV training on this day.

Perform each exercise to MMF within eight to ten repetitions unless otherwise indicated. Do three sets of each. Rest between sets for forty-five seconds. As always, begin with a ten-minute active warm-up.

Workout A

Superset:
Stiff Leg Deadlifts with Back Squats. Assume a narrow stance on both.

Superset:
Leg Curls with Jump Squats or Scissor Jumps. You may wish to perform four sets, thereby allowing two sets of each of the latter.

Superset:
Powercleans. Upon failure of good form and/or the completion of the required reps, immediately "polish off" the set by performing Shrugs to failure.

Dips	If you are using added weight to failure within the required 8-10 reps, then the last set should be a "Breakaway Set."
Seated Press	Take your pick of DBs, barbell, or machine.

Lying Triceps Extensions	Watch your form as always, remain super strict with this one.
Barbell Curls	See same notation as above exercise.
Standing Calf Raises	Do 4-5 sets here.
Superset	Reach Thru's with some type of Leg Raises (lying, suspended, hanging). Do each for 1:00.
DB Swings	Do 3x1:00. Keep shoulders low and relaxed. Concentrate on frequency and rhythm.

Workout B

Perform three sets of each exercise for eighteen to twenty reps unless otherwise indicated. The rest phase is the same as in Workout A.

Stiff Leg Deadlifts

Superset:
Leg Press with GP Squats. Pick your type of Leg Press.

Superset:
Leg Curls with Ski Stance.

Superset:
Front Lat Pulldowns with Bent Arm Pullovers. Use a pullover machine if possible. Vary grip and width on the Pulldowns. Change bars if available.

Superset:
Bench Press with Side Lateral Raises.

Superset:
Pressdowns with Two-Bench Triceps. Carry the latter to failure at bodyweight.

Seated Alternating DB Curls

Seated Calf Raises.

Superset:
Twist Crunches with Russian Twists.

Abdominal Wheel for up to: 3x1:00. Hook heels if needed.

DAY TWO

This is your CV and Flexibility Training day. One one Day Two workout, perform a high-intensity, low-volume type of workout (like RollerBlade intervals, for example), then on the next Day Two, do a low-intensity/high-volume workout (like going out for a long mountain bike ride or a run). Be creative. The flexibility session should be no less than thirty minutes of conscientious relaxation.

FIRST TRANSITION PHASE (BACKCOUNTRY SKIING)

This phase should begin approximately one and a half to two months before ski season begins.

Prescription:
Follow the program design as described in the OFF-SEASON routines with the following alterations:

A COMPOSITE ROUTINE DAY needs to be integrated into the cycle. For example, if you are following the first OFF-SEASON CYCLE (a three-day cycle), a training week should now look like this:

Monday	Strength Training; Lower Body, Workout A
Tuesday	Strength Training; Upper Body, Workout A
Wednesday	Recovery Day from Strength Training, long CV and Flexibility Training day
Thursday	Strength Training; Composite Routine
Friday	Same as Wednesday
Saturday & Sunday	You can now: (1) Begin cycle over again using Workout B, OR (2) Take the weekend away from training to do specific sport activity and begin Workout B cycle on Monday.

During this First Transition Phase, the Strength Day can be eliminated.

ON-SEASON TRAINING FOR BACKCOUNTRY SKIING

During this period, the athlete is concerned primarily with the maintenance of his conditioning level. Indoor training is minimized, attempting instead to spend as much time as possible on the snow. I suggest coming into the gym for strength training two times every five to seven days. These "in-gym" training days should be non-consecutive and alternate between the two strength-training prescriptions which follow. CV Training needs a high priority during this phase and should be creatively pursued on each non-strength training day, and also on days when skiing is not possible. The minimum CV training should be thirty minutes at a moderate intensity. Flexibility training should be performed two times per week minimum for a full-body session lasting thirty minutes.

A member of the Women's U.S. Ski Team doing some strength-specific training for cross-country racing.

STRENGTH-TRAINING PROGRAMS:
ON-SEASON WORKOUT A

Each set should be carried to MMF within six to eight reps unless indicated otherwise. Do three sets each. Limit rest between sets to forty-five seconds or less. Begin with a ten-minute active warm-up.

Back Squats

Split Jumps	3x10-12 jumps
Leg Curls	With Ilg variant if possible
Pullups	Alternative, Front Lat Pulldowns
Dips	Add weight when necessary

Seated Barbell Press

Narrow Grip Barbell Press

Barbell Curls

Standing Calf Raise

Abdominal Work	Use experiential discretion for exercise choice. Pick two movements; perform 3x1:00 of each.

Workout B, On-Season

Follow the exercise prescription given for the COMPOSITE PROGRAM on this day.

A Training Program for the Recreational Hiker and Backpacker

Hikers and backpackers practice an outdoor art of the most extraordinary therapeutical degree. Many of history's most powerful thinkers cherished regular excursions into the out-of-doors. Some thought they were vital. I give you Tim Boyer and Ginger Oppenheimer and their feelings: "The things we like best in wilderness are transitory; evening light, sunrises and sunsets, fall colors, strong winds, storms, lightning, new snow, full moons, and more. The essence of all things is the moment. They happen, and to experience them, to see them, we need to be in the right place with the right attitude."

I have offered below both "on" and "off" season training programs which may be followed as seasonal and/or activity levels dictate.

I think that better conditioning through these programs will help you discover another meaning to that precious "right attitude."

MOVEMENT PATTERNS OF THE BACKPACKER

Knee Lift Phase: As the knee is brought skyward, the hip flexors and hip extensors are our primary initiators. Musculature: psoas, iliacus (iliopsoas), and the gluteal complex.

The Pulling Phase: As the lead leg makes ground contact, it is rear thigh musculature responsible for pulling the body up to the push-off phase. A strength coach friend has referred to this phase as the "Pawing Phase."

The Push-Off Phase: As the body passes over the lead leg, extension of this leg must occur. Forward progress is made by the frontal thigh musculature (quadriceps). In the latter part of this phase, the foot orchestrates effective "blast-off" force. This is done by the calf muscles.

The concept of athletic transfer: Which do you think is more comfortable? — A Lowe Expedition pack with fifty-five pounds, or a York Olympic bar with over twice that amount? Answers provided at the end of your "Off-Season" training.

ADDENDUM FOR BACKPACKERS

For heavily laden hikers, concern for greater stress is to be grasped. The pulling phase is under greater stress due to an upper torso angle change. Contraction of back and buttock (gluteal) musculature is greatly needed for stabilization of "pack swing." This ongoing contraction must be handled via abdominal and hip, back, shoulder, and neck musculature. Terrain incongruities also necessitate adequate knee and ankle stabilization.

EXERCISE PRESCRIPTION FOR HIKERS AND BACKPACKERS: OFF-SEASON

Follow a three-day cycle. Perform ten minutes of an active warm-up before strength training. Limit rest between sets to forty-five seconds. Do not rest with supersets. Lift fluidly and in good tempo. Explosive positive phases should be countered by slower, controlled negative phases. A set is not a set until MMF has been reached.

DAY ONE

— Strength Training —

Back Squats	Alternates include: Hacke Squat machines or Front Squats, 3x8-10
Superset: Jump Squats with GP Squats	Do 30 seconds of Jump Squats and then immediately go to 60 seconds worth of elegantly done GP Squats. Do that for 3 sets.
Pullups	Do as many as you can. As your repetitions increase, keep an open mind toward elegance in form.
Dips	Same thoughts as with Pullups.
2-Way Ilgs	2-3 sets of 8-10 on the first phase, then "rep out" (do as many reps as possible in good form) on the second phase.
Seated Press	3x8-10. Do most of your training here with a barbell.
Lying Triceps Extensions	4x10-12 would be fantastic.
Seated Alternating DB Curls	Really twist the wrist outward up top. Keep shoulders relaxed, do not involve them. 4x10-12 each arm.
Superset: Seated Calf Raises with Stiff Leg Deadlifts	Reach MMF with 15 reps on the calves, then use moderate resistance on the "Stiff Legs" for the same number of reps. Do this superset three to four times.

Abdominal Crunches   Alternate would be Reach Thru's.
                            3x30-60 seconds. Concentrate, feel the
                            abdominals; make the crunch up in the
                            top position.

— Other Training —

If time and energy permit, a CV Training session of no more than
twenty to thirty minutes would be great. The intensity should be
high, however. An optimal choice would be running stadium stairs
or uphill sprints for thirty or sixty seconds each.

DAY TWO

Training should be centered around a long, low-intensity CV excur-
sion. This can be a hike, bike ride, jog, or whatever blend you
choose. Go for at least sixty minutes. A Flexibility Training session
of no less than thirty minutes needs to be done on this day also.

DAY THREE

— Strength Training —

Perform each of the following exercises for thirty seconds, attempting to reach MMF at the thirty-second point. Do three sets of each
before moving on to the next exercise.

(1) Leg Press

(2) Leg Curls Superset with Seated Good Mornings

(3) Stepups, 2 sets only

(4) Front Lat Pulldowns Superset with DB Shrugs

(5) Bench Press or DB Flyes

(6) Upright Rows or DB Side Lateral Raises

(7) Two-Bench Triceps Superset with Barbell Curls

(8) Holding Reach Thru's Superset with Leg Raises

(9) Standing Calf Raises

— Other Training —

Ideally, this day would include some form of Kinesthetic Training, examples being a ballet, gymnastics, or aerobics class.

HIKERS AND BACKPACKERS: ON-SEASON TRAINING

During the active on-season, the majority of backpackers will maximize weekends for their outdoor pursuits. Maintenance of conditioning levels during this phase is acquired by training in the following manner:

Day One	Take an Active Rest Day following the excursion.
Day Two	Strength train on the COMPOSURE PROGRAM given at the beginning of this section.
Day Three	Perform a CV and Flexibility Training session of moderate intensity, long duration (30 minutes minimum).
Day Four	Strength train on the COMPOSITE PROGRAM given at the beginning of this section.
Day Five	Do some form of Kinesthetic Training as described above. Flexibility Training, 10 minutes minimum.
Days Six and Seven	Sport-specific activity.

The mountain bike, an all-terrain, all-seasonal approach for the outdoor athlete. *Photo by David Langdon.*

Exercise Prescription for Mountain Bikers

Mountain biking has recently experienced a popularity explosion. Higher technology has enabled able cyclists to explore bi-wheeled adventure in terrain untouched to previous generations of cyclists. Conditioning for the mountain biker is not dissimilar to that of the road cyclist, the exception being a greater emphasis on kinesthetic coordination and upper torso strength.

The avid mountain biker is in danger of developing knee problems caused by long rides on steep climbs. The frontal thighs are often overworked compared to the rear thigh. This can result in a common muscle imbalance. In addition to promoting unified muscular poise, training improves explosive power for the uphills. Also, training by the suggested guidelines below help you develop what I call "dynamic balance," which is the ability to control your body while in motion.

MAJOR MOVEMENT PATTERNS

While seated or upright, the primary pedal stroke occurs during hip and leg extension and flexion. The hip's foremost extensors are the gluteals and to a lesser degree, the hamstrings or rear thigh. The flexion phase or the follow-through motion is accomplished by contraction of the iliposoas, hamstrings, and lower gluteus (minimus). Action of the foot is important to smooth recovery and a balanced pedal stroke. This is done by the calf musculature. Postural alignment is imperative to the mountain biker; therefore, well-developed abdominals and back erectors must be adequately trained. "Working" the handlebars calls for strength in the latissimus dorsi, trapezius, and bicep musculature.

Below is a program designed for year-round use. Use the Three-Day Cycle for BUILDING of strength levels specific to mountain biking. For MAINTENANCE of conditioning levels, follow the COMPOSITE PROGRAM twice weekly on non-consecutive days, spending as much time as possible on the bike or an aerobic alternative. The COMPOSITE PROGRAM is given earlier in this section.

THREE-DAY CYCLE

DAY ONE

— Strength Training —

Exercise	Workout A	Workout B
Warm-up	10 minutes	10 minutes
Back Squats	5x8-10	None
Front Squats	None	3x12-15
Touch 'n Go Lunges	None	3x12-15
Superset: Leg Press with Leg Extensions	3x15 of each	None
Step-ups	3x10-12	None
Split Jumps	None	3x10-12
Leg Curls	5x15x30	4x8-10
Stiff Leg Deadlifts	2x15	2x15
Standing Calf Raises	None	4x1:00
Seated Calf Raises	3x8-10	None

— CV Training —

Moderate volume, moderate intensity.

— Flexibility Training —

If time permits, fifteen to thirty minutes.

DAY TWO

— Strength Training —

Exercise	Workout A	Workout B
Warm-up		
Hangcleans	3x8-10	None
2-Way Ilgs	None	3x10-12 each phase
Pullups	3x?	None
Pulldowns to Behind the Neck	None	3x12-15
Bench Press	None	3x12-15
Dips	3x?	None
A L.C.M.	2x10-12	2x2:00
Seated Press	2-3x8-10	None
DB Side Lateral Raises	None	2-3x12-15
Lying Tricep Extension	4x8-10	None

Pressdown	None	4x12-15
Barbell Curls	4x6-8	None
Alt. Seated DB Curls	None	4x12-15
Superset: Reach-Thru's and Leg Raises	3x1:00 of each	None
Russian Twists	None	3x12-15
Abdominal Wheel or Twist Crunches	None	3x1:00

— CV Training —

Low-volume, high-intensity; an interval workout, for example.

DAY THREE

Off from strength training. Perform at least two of the following activities:

(A) Long-duration CV Training session

(B) A Flexibility Training session for thirty minutes

(C) A form of Kinesthetic Training

Note: Mountain bikers will also benefit from the forearm exercises described on page 112.

Reading a watery language and allowing it to pitch and toss athletic intent.

Exercise Prescriptions for Kayakers and Paddlers

"In Xanadu did Kubla Khan
A stately pleasure-dome decree:
Where Alph, the sacred river, ran
Through caverns measureless to man
Down to sunless sea.

— from Kubla Khan, *Samuel Taylor Coleridge*

Release. Surrendering. At time pressuring. At other times, coercing. Reading a watery language and allowing it to pitch and toss one's athletic intent. Brushing hydrogen and oxygen atoms with sensitivity and rhythm.

If any outdoor pursuit demands rhythm and a devotion to active surrender, it surely must be the white water sports. Where I grew up, swollen creeks turned with seasonal rapidity into furious rivers filled with quotidian adventure. On all fours, perched atop a quivering inner-tube of dubious strength. Headlong my buddies and I would spin into the grand flexions and churnings of some flooding glacial arm.

Kids.

Yet, within those pubescent days of danger, there was great beauty and a richness to life. We can again be touched by this splendor. The key comes in the form of canoes, rafts, and kayaks.

The athletic prowess needed for these water pursuits is evident. ". . . The arms, shoulders, wrists, and hands are undergoing quite a bit of strain when balancing and paddling the boat . . . A paddler can become quite weary after thirty minutes or so of sitting in a kayak. The importance of good physical condition and proper muscle tone is strikingly emphasized." — From the *Digest Book of Canoes, Kayaks, and Rafts*, by Charles J. Farmer.

MAJOR MOVEMENT PATTERNS

The pulling motion of paddling and stroking happens by way of the trapezius and latissimus dorsi of the back, the deltoids of the shoulder, and the biceps of the arm. Follow-through is an extension by the triceps. Recovery and "dip" is accomplished by the deltoids and trapezius of the shoulder and triceps.

Stabilization of effectual body position is needed. The back and sides must be trained, focusing effort to the erector spinae, obliques, and abdominals.

PERIODZATIONAL METHODOLOGY

I suggest that the white water athlete's training year be divided into two distinct phases. The first is the Strength Building Phase or, as we will call it, the OFF-SEASON PHASE. It is during this period that the physiological components of muscle strength and power, muscle endurance, flexibility, and CV are trained with high priority. An OFF-SEASON program is given below.

As sport-specific activity increases, conditioning levels are to be maintained. This phase can be known as the ON-SEASON.

During such a high activity period, the following training protocol can be considered:

Perform strength-training exercises as per the COMPOSITE PROGRAM given earlier in this section. This should be done twice weekly on non-consecutive days. CV Training, as well as Flexibility and Kinesthetic Training, are to be done once or twice a week for thirty minutes. The CV Training should be of moderate intensity.

OFF-SEASON STRENGTH-BUILDING EXERCISE PRESCRIPTION (KAYAKERS AND PADDLERS)

DAY ONE

— Strength Training —

Exercise	Workout A	Workout B
Warm-up	8-10 minutes	8-10 minutes
Back Squats	3x8-10	None
Front Squats	None	3x12-15
Superset: Ski Stance with GP Squats	3x1:00 each	None
Touch 'n Go Lunges	None	3x10-12
Adductor Exercise	2-3x10-12	See Workout A

Leg Curls	3x8-10	5x15x30
Superset: Standing Calf Raises with Stiff Leg Deadlifts	3x8-10	3x1:00

— CV Training —

High-intensity, low-volume workout. Example stationary cycle workout: Five minutes hard effort, five minutes easy effort; follow this principle for thirty minutes.

DAY TWO

— Strength Training —

Exercise	Workout A	Workout B
Warm-up	Should include repetition jerks, 3x10-12 done with moderate poundage.	
Bent-Arm Pullovers	3x10-12	None
Narrow Grip Pulldowns	None	3x10-12
2-Way Ilgs	3x8-10	None
Under Grip Pullups or Pulldowns	None	3x10-12

Dips or DB Bench Press	3x8-10	None
DB or Machine Flyes	None	3x10-12
Seated Press	3x8-10	None
Side Lateral Raises	None	3x10-12, "lsd"
Lying Triceps Extension	3x8-10	3x8-10
DB Kickbacks	3x10-12	None
Pressdowns	None	3x10-12
Barbell Curls	3x8-10	None
Seated Alt. DB Curls	None	3x10-12
Superset: (A) Reverse Wrist Curls with (B) Wrist Curls	3x(A)12-15, (B)8-10	
Russian Twists	3x1:00	None
Holding Reach Thru's	3x25	None
Endurance Situps	None	4-5x1:00

— Other Training —

None.

DAY THREE

— CV Training —

Thirty to forty-five minutes, moderate intensity.

— Flexibility Training —

Ten to thirty minutes.

— Kinesthetic Training —

Discretionary.

Exercise Prescription for Surfers and Skiers

Compatible Activities: Downhill Skiing, Wave Sailing/Jumping, Speed Sailing, Water Skiing, Hang Gliding, Ice Surfing

In this genus of outdoor sports, a bright and shiny common denominator surfaces. Dynamic balance. All of windsurfing is change. Should the athlete become rigid in any way, shape, or form,

Windsurfing: Allowing fluidity of change to become your composition. *Photo by David Langdon.*

death is certain. So if our axiom be this kinesthetic fusion, training must be drawn inward. The finer grained nuances of Strength Training must be embraced, as well as CV Training for efficient heart and respiratory systems. While the former offers the surfer effective strength, the latter allows for a physiology resilient to fatigue.

PERIODZATIONAL TRAINING METHODOLOGY

Follow the same guidelines as offered for kayakers and other paddlers.

MAJOR MOVEMENT PATTERNS

The primary movement, especially if harness technique is not being engaged, is hanging. Advanced 'surfers recognize the value of "getting off" the musculature by hanging, relaxed but alertly, on the skeleton. However, where there is a hang, there is a pull. This blending of hanging and pulling is accomplished by contraction of the latissimus dorsi and trapezius of the central and upper back, and biceps and deltoids of the upper arms and shoulders, respectively. Lateral pulls and motions, cross-pressure strengths, and balancing pulls can occur via the pectoralis muscles of the chest.

Stabilization throughout the body comes from contractions of the midsection: Abdominals, erector spinae, and obliques. Lower body balance depends largely upon the isometric contraction of the gluteus, and flexors and extensors of the hips, as well as the abductors and adductors of the legs. Control of the board is orchestrated by strong calves and feet which are responsible for plantar and dorsi flexion movements.

OFF-SEASON EXERCISE PRESCRIPTION, THREE-DAY ALTERNATING CYCLE (SURFERS AND SKIERS)

DAY ONE

— Strength Training —

Workout A:
Perform three sets of eight to ten repetitions to MMF in each exercise unless noted otherwise.

Workout B:
Perform three sets of twelve to fifteen repetitions to MMF in each exercise unless noted otherwise. Limit rest to forty-five seconds between all sets and exercises.

As always, perform an active warm-up for approximately ten minutes. Jump roping, and learning new "tricks" while doing so, is a suggested example.

Workout A	Workout B
Back Squats	Superset: Leg Press with GP Squats
Side or Touch 'n Go Lunges	Jump Squats, 30 seconds
Leg Curls	Ski Stance, 3x1:00
Adductor Machine or variant	Superset: Stiff Leg Deadlifts with Leg Curls
Side Jumps	Standing Calf Raises
Seated Calf Raises or variant	

— CV Training —

If time permits, do five sets of 2:00 worth of interval type of training. The manner is discretionary (stationary cycling, jogging, rowing, etc.). You should be completely recovered before beginning the next interval. The interval should be of high-intensity effort.

DAY TWO

Workout A

Hang Cleans or 2-Way Ilgs
3x8-10

Pullups, as many as possible

Dips, 3x8-10

Incline Bench Press, 2x8-10

Seated Press, 2x8-10

Lying Triceps Extensions,
3x8-10

Pressdowns, 2x12-15

Barbell Curls, 3x8-10

Superset, 3x: Reverse Wrist
Curls (20-25) with Wrist
Curls (8-10)

Workout B

Seated Rows with a hold in
top position, 3x:30 seconds

Undergrip Pullups, as many
as possible

L.C.M., 3x:30 seconds

Incline Bench Press, 2x:30
seconds

Repetition Jerks, 2x10-12

2-Bench Triceps, 3x1:00

DB Kickbacks, 1-2x:30
seconds

Seated Alternating DB Curls,
4x:30 seconds

Exercise Prescription for 'Boarders

Compatible Activities: Surfboarding, Skateboarding, Snowboarding

Plato is attributed with once saying, "The most beautiful motion is that which accomplishes the greatest results with the least amount of effort."

To the beginner, there is great physicalness in boarding activities. After a time, a living pulse is sensed by the athlete under his feet. The board has created the skillfulness; it has studied the surface through itself and already knows its own elegance. The rider re-

On the surf, or asphalt, a 'boarder's primary movement patterns are similar and should be trained. *Photo by Fran Richards.*

sponds to this pulse. All of training, therefore, must be designed to do away with fatigue. To build a better body more capable of efficient body position which promotes fluidity when riding. It really matters little the surface upon which one chooses to board. Be it sea, sand, asphalt, or snow, all that remains to sport performance improvement is "fluid" strength and "reading" the surface language.

MAJOR MOVEMENT PATTERNS

Reread carefully this category under EXERCISE PRESCRIPTION FOR WINDSURFERS. Much of 'boarding equates to neuromuscular patterns which have been made more efficient through practice. In the upper torso, the trunk is critical for conduction of lower body forces. The contractions of the abdominals, obliques, and lower back are continuous and provide authoritative balance when sheer dynamics of the sport require utmost stabilization. Lower body balance is dictated by powerful and delicate contractions occurring in the quadriceps and hamstrings of the legs and hips, as well as the "fine tuning" musculature of the foot movements. Muscles responsible for this latter action are the gastrocnemius, and the soleus of the rear calf, and the tibialis/peroneus of the shin area.

PERIODZATIONAL TRAINING METHODOLOGY

Follow the same Periodzational Training guidelines as are given for kayakers and other paddlers.

OFF-SEASON TRAINING, 3-DAY CYCLE ('BOARDERS)

Insert one COMPOSITE PROGRAM workout every seven days. All sets to MMF as dictated by the sets and repetitions. Limit rest between sets to forty-five seconds. Alternate workouts each cycle.

DAY ONE

Exercise	WorkoutA	Workout B
Active Warm-Up, 10 minutes		
Side Hops (see Squat Jumps for description)	2x10-12 jumps	None
Split Jumps	None	2x10-12
Superset for 3 sets: (A) Squat jumps with (B) GP Squats	None	(A) 30 seconds (B) 1:00
Back Squats	4x12-15	None
Adductor Work	3x8-10	None
Superset for 3 sets: Leg Curls with Stiff Leg Deadlifts	8-10 of each	12-15 of each
Ski Stance	3x1:00-2:00	None
Touch 'n Go Lunges	None	3x10-12
Standing Calf Raises	4x8-10	None
Seated Calf Raises	None	4x15-20

— CV Training —

Thirty minutes of low to moderate intensity.

— **Flexibility Training** —

Ten minutes minimum.

DAY TWO

Exercise	Workout A	Workout B
Hang Cleans	3x8-10	None
2-Way Ilgs	None	3x10-12
Pullups or Front Lat Pulldowns	3x8-10	None
Seated Rows	None	5x15x30
Dips	3x8-10	None
Bench Press or a L.C.M.	None	3x10-12
Superset 2x: Seated Press with Side Lateral Raises	8-10/12-15	None
Repetition Jerks	None	3x12-15
Superset 2x: Lying Triceps Extensions with 2-Bench Triceps	None	8-10/?
Pressdowns	4x8-10 "1sd"	None
DB Kickbacks	2x12-15	2x8-10

Barbell Curls	4x8-10	None
Seated Alt. DB Curls	None	4x12-15
Reach Thru's	2x1:00	2x1:00
Russian Twists	3x12-15	None
Abdominal Wheel	None	3x1:00
Suspended Leg Raises	3x30 seconds	3x15 with throw-downs

— Other Training —

Some type of Kinesthetic Training if possible.

DAY THREE

Off from Strength Training. Make this an active day and keep a low-caloric intake. A long CV and Flexibility Training session is strongly urged. Some form of Kinesthetic Training is also attempted on this day.

The underwater athlete enjoys an arena filled with surrealistic and ever-changing splendor. *Photo by Steve Weaver, Courtesy of Weaver Dive Shop, Boulder, Colorado.*

Exercise Prescription for Swimmers, Snorkelers, and Other Water-Rats

Compatible Activities: Scuba Diving, Distance/Adventure Swimming

Swimmers, especially underwater swimmers, inhabit a world contrary to the more "normal" world of sun and sky. Their playground is one of surrealistic and ever-changing effect. It is one of silence and filled with fine swirls of muted character. One learns to communicate succinctly in a sensual language whether the rapport be with friends, the surroundings, or with one's self. Keeping an open, alert awareness is imperative. Danger is evident. Physiological accidents offer frightening possibilities: Air embolism, overexpansion of internal organs, and other compressed-air-induced illnesses. Training can afford a backdrop of physical preparation which is a comforting, if not vital, dimension.

All motion done in water requires a special type of strength. Not only is there great stress on the cardiovascular and cardiorespiratory systems, but also the strength demands are unique in that eccentric contractions of the muscles are rare. The action of the swimmer, therefore, is push, pull, recover. Propulsion is derived from lift forces which are produced by vertical and lateral motions of the arms and legs. Competitive swimmers who I have trained have found much success by gearing strength-training programs to emphasize explosive moments. Such training leads to quicker limb recovery, which, in turn, maximizes arm and leg stroke power.

MAJOR MOVEMENT PATTERNS

Owing to the diversity of strokes, the program below emphasizes general strengths. This allows for effective strength transfer into specific strengths. Rest assured that strength training must be aimed at the following bodyparts: The latissimus dorsi, trapezius, and teres complex of the back; the pectoralis muscles of the chest; and the deltoid complex, biceps and triceps brachii, brachialis, and brachioradialis of the shoulders, upper arms, and forearms, respectively. Nearly all of the lower body musculature is involved; the gluteals of the buttocks, the quadriceps of the frontal thigh, the bicep femoris, semitendonosus, semimembranosus, and the adductor complex of the rear, middle, and inner thigh, respectively. Foot position is accomplished by hip involvement (gluteals and the illipsoas) and more directly by an offsetting action of the rear calf musculature, the soleus and gastrocnemius, and of the frontal calf musculature including the peroneus complex and the tibialis anterior. Finally, a well-developed abdominal region provides the swimmer with proper body position through increased stabilization. Muscles responsible for this are the rectus abdominus and the obliques.

PERIODZATIONAL METHODOLOGY

Follow the same Periodzational Training guidelines as are given for kayakers and other paddlers.

OFF-SEASON TRAINING PRESCRIPTION, 5-DAY CYCLE (SWIMMERS, SNORKELERS, AND OTHER WATER RATS)

DAY ONE

— Strength Training —

This full-body workout is designed to improve power for the swimmer. All exercises should be carried to MMF within six reps except where noted otherwise. Do three sets of each exercise. Recovery time between sets and exercises should be no more than 2:00. Perform an active warm-up for at least ten minutes before strength training is begun. Warm-up should include: Jump Squats, 3x10-12, and Split Jumps, 3x10-12.

(1) Back Squats

(2) Full Deadlifts

(3) Powercleans

(4) Bench Press

(5) Repetition Jerks (Experienced lifters: Power Snatches)

(6) Lying Triceps Extensions

(7) Barbell Curls

(8) Twist Crunches, 3x25

— CV Training —

Efficient breathing patterns are crucial for enjoyment and safety to the swimmer. Strength Training and CV Training done at high intensities for short time periods (Interval Training) will improve the athlete's respiratory fitness. Additionally, interval training has been shown to induce a low oxygen level in the muscles. Interval training can "teach" the muscles to remain functional under such oxygen-deprived conditions.

Pick a form of CV Training (swimming, jogging, etc.) and perform at a high intensity of effort for two to three minutes. Try to recover and go again within the same amount of time. Do a minimum of three sets.

DAY TWO

— Strength Training —

None. Recovery day.

— CV Training —

Thirty minutes minimum at low to moderate intensity.

— Flexibility Training —

Fifteen minutes, full body.

DAY THREE

— Strength Training —

Perform 3x12-15 to MMF of each exercise except where noted otherwise. Limit recovery periods to forty-five seconds. Active warm-up for ten minutes prior to strength training.

(1) Superset: Leg Presses with GP Squats

(2) Touch 'n Go Lunges

(3) Superset: Leg Extensions or Hacke Squats with Leg Curls

(4) Superset: Stiff Leg Deadlifts with Calf Raises (vary)

DAY FOUR

— Strength Training —

Same notations as in DAY THREE

(1) Hang Cleans
   Alternative: Narrow Grip Pulldowns or Seated Rows

(2) Pullups
   Alternative: Undergrip Pullups, Front Lat Pulldowns

(3) Dips: Do as many as possible

(4) Flyes, 2 sets

(5) Repetition Jerks, 1 set

(6) Superset: Seated Press (vary) with Side Lateral Raises,
   2 supersets

(7) Superset: Pressdowns with Seated Alternating DB Curls

(8) Superset: Russian Twists with Leg Raises (vary)

(9) Tennis Ball Squeeze or Alternative. Squeeze at rapid tempo,
   3x1:00.

DAY FIVE

Follow guidelines given on Day Two.

"Now my soul hath elbow room." —Shakespeare. *Photo courtesy of Dave Felkley.*

Exercise Prescription for Adventure Runners

Compatible Activities: Mountain Running, PowerHiking, PowerWalking

> *"Now my soul hath elbow-room."*
> — *Shakespeare*

My first pair of "running" shoes were Converse Hi-Tops. They seemed to complement the rest of my typical running garb: Blue jeans, flannel shirt, and a Rossignol ski cap all offset by a large-buckled cowboy belt.

I ran for an unknown. I ran because I was little and fast and I lived out, way out, in the mountains of southwestern Colorado. In those pre-GoreTex days, inclement weather reduced my runs to hikes. Little did I care; the countless miracles of a world encumbered by nothing at all showed to me, at a tender age, that it was okay to love running for movement's sake. And nothing else.

I know why we run, and the reason is infinitely deeper than the words convey: We adventure run because we know that fun is always just up, over, and around the next horizon.

MAJOR MOVEMENT PATTERNS AND CONSIDERATIONS

Most "normal" running is accomplished via a methodical and closely guarded logical cadence. It is with mathematical precision and a regulated rhythm that the footfalls of the street runner are fashioned.

Conversely, the adventure runner operates at the whimsical vagaries of the great unknown, Mother Nature. Each foot plant is a sum of instinct and foresight. The terrain is everchanging; sometimes rocky and rutty, at other times smooth and slippery. Stride length adjustments are often made in milliseconds. Increased knee lift is a response to uphill onslaughts. Hips and upper body sway to attenuate depressions. Arm swing acts as a counterweight to correct subtle imbalances forced by tenacious terrain.

In a technical vein, the adventure runner depends primarily upon endurance. Slow twitch muscle fiber units, the ones resilient to fatigue, are a biological blessing. However, the concept of power, that ability to generate forceful muscular contractions, cannot go unheralded. A power-trained runner will discover the uphills more of a friend and less of an enemy.

The musculature driving the power train of the all-terrain runner are the legs and hips. The gluteals of the buttocks and the ilipsoas assume duty here. For an authoritative push-off motion, the upper leg via the quadriceps and the lower leg via the rear calf muscles extend their patronage to this aspect.

Arm drive is important. A strong arm carriage gives good cadence. The deltoid complex of the shoulder as well as the trapezius of the upper back should be well trained. Follow through of arm swing is created by the biceps and brachialis.

To maintain upper body position, which allows for greater force potentiation of leg and hip drive, training is targeted for the lower back and the frontal and side abdominal musculature.

PERIODZATIONAL TRAINING METHODOLOGY

Follow the same Periodzational Training guidelines as are given for kayakers and other paddlers.

OFF-SEASON TRAINING PRESCRIPTION, 3-DAY CYCLE (ADVENTURE RUNNERS)

DAY ONE

Perform each set to MMF as dictated by the repetitions. Limit rest between sets to forty-five seconds. Alternate workouts A and B to every three-day cycle. Insert a COMPOSITE PROGRAM every seven days. Remember that active warm-up precedes each strength-training session.

— Strength Training —

Exercise	Workout A	Workout B
Back Squats	3x8-10	None
Front Squats	None	3x8-10
Scissor Jumps	3x10-12	None
Superset 3x: Squat Jumps with GP Squats	None	30 seconds/1:00
Leg Press	3x15-20	5x15x30
Superset 3x: Leg Curls with Stiff Leg Deadlifts	15 of each	6-8 of each
Side Hops (optional)	2x12	2x12
Calf Raises (vary)	4x8-10	4x1:00

— CV Training —

Interval training of your discretion. Five to ? sets of 2:00 high-intensity work. Recovery period, two to three minutes.

— Other Training —

Time permitting: A Kinesthetic and/or Flexibility Training session would be beneficial on this day.

DAY TWO

— Strength Training —

Exercise	Workout A	Workout B
Hang Cleans	3x8-10	None
2-Way Ilgs	None	3x8-10
Pullups	3x? (BW)	3x? (BW)
Dips or Bench Press	3x8-10	None
A L.C.M.	None	3x12-15
Seated Press	3x8-10	None
Repetition Jerks	None	3x30 seconds
Superset 4x: Lying Triceps Extension with Barbell Curls	8-10 of each	None
Superset 3x: Pressdowns with 2-Bench Triceps	None	8-10/? (BW)
Seated Alt. DB Curls	2x1:00	4x8-10
DB Swings	2x1:00	4x30 seconds
Superset 3x: Russian Twists with Reach Thru's		15/1:00
Leg Raises (vary)	4x1:00	None
Abdominal Wheel	2?x1:00?	None

— CV Training —

Discretionary. Moderate intensity and volume.

DAY THREE

— Strength Training —

None. Recovery day.

— CV Training —

High volume/moderate to high intensity.

— Flexibility Training —

Mandatory. Do a minimum of fifteen to thirty minutes, full-body.

Part III

Exercise Essentials: Training Movements Illustrated

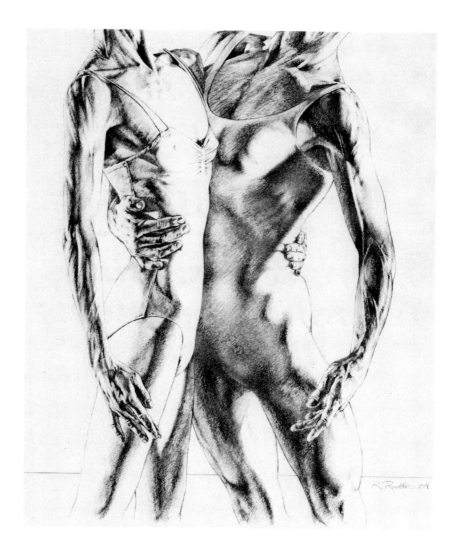

Training Movements

"When ideas fail, words come in very handy."

— *Goethe*

I have done my best to bring you my ideas in a style conducive to personal interpretation. Perhaps when polished by enough training sessions, these individual images not only will become sharper and clearer, but also more variably meaningful. I give you the following pages as hints, not statements. Not "how-to" pages (there are plenty of those in other books . . .), but "what-if" suggestions. The following basics may offer clarity to earlier words, yet it remains your responsibility to discover, should you seek them, the truths which exist, limitless, beyond each movement.

Have fun.

Photographs by David Langdon. Softwear: Bottoms by Original Skins, Top by Street Closed. Footwear by Tiger.

The Warm-Up

Left: Stationary cycling as an active warm-up. The active warm-up is a prerequisite to all strength-training sessions. Eight to ten minutes of moderate intensity helps insure against muscle pulls and serves many physiological and psychological purposes needed for a good workout. *Right:* Dumbbell swings. This is an excellent upper body warm-up exercise that has direct positive inroads to athletic performance. These first few moments of warming the body should be a joyful celebration of circulating energy, the re-awaking of one's spirit and a needed hush to a noisy mind.

Lower Body

Back Squats

Left: Start position — Do this exercise; it will change your life. *Right:* Bottom position — Up and down, piston-like, never retarding the flow of the set.

MOVEMENT

From start, a slow negative phase until the top of the thigh is parallel to the floor. A smooth, forceful transition initiates the powerful, explosive positive phase which is carried through to start position.

ABSTRACTS

All of the poetic and gritty power of strength training is found within the world of the Back Squat. No other exercise opens as many doors to improved performance than Squats. It is here that one begins the pursuit of perfect integration; rhythmic style, flowing breathing patterns, focalization of all energy to the bodypart(s). Up and down, piston-like, never retarding the flow of the set. Lower back is always flat, and nearly vertical. Bar is placed low on the upper back. In the top (start) position, knees ARE NEVER FULLY EXTENDED! A "locked out" joint removes muscular tension, diminishes the training effect, and can be harmful instead of beneficial to joint health. Stance can be varied, but heels must remain connected to the floor. Toes point slightly outward, knees track in that same angle.

ASPECTS

All of the lower body. Stabilization of movement will train the entire body in a dynamic manner.

RELATED MOVEMENTS

Front Squats: Bar is placed in front of the neck and held there, as in the finish position of the PowerClean.

Hacke Squats: Done on a Hacke Machine, this removes some buttock (gluteal) emphasis and shifts in to the frontal thigh.

Jump Squats

Left: Start position — The mindset is one of speed and body control. *Right:* Mid position — Upon landing, the athlete concentrates on a reaction to the ground.

MOVEMENT

Bodyweight only. Begin similar to the bottom position of a Back Squat. Interlock fingers and place the hands behind the head. Explode upward as high as possible. Upon landing, do your best to get off the ground as fast as possible.

ABSTRACTS

This is a plyometric exercise, one designed to increase explosive power. The mindset is one of speed and body control. Quality is always more important than quantity in power-training movements. Back stays flat, head and chest remain forward. Breathe deeply and fully; exhalation occurs on the upward explosion.

ASPECTS

The basic power developer. Trains the hip flexors, quadriceps, calf muscles, hamstrings, and the gluteal muscles.

RELATED MOVEMENTS

Side Hops: Place two cones or the likeness thereof (about two feet in height), two to three feet apart. Side hops involve performing the basics of a Squat Jump but jumping sideways over the cones. Change directions.

Split Jumps

Left: Start position — These develop power and motor skill control. *Right:* Mid position — "In this brief transit where the dreams cross. . ." — *T.S. Elliot.*

MOVEMENT

From the start position, jump as high as possible while maintaining upper body erectness. At the apex of the jump (mid position), legs are brought together, then quickly return to anticipate the landing. Regain stability, jump again. One leg is trained at a time.

ABSTRACTS

An intermediate plyometric movement. Apply softness and rigidity in learning the action sequence. There is balance in breath; do not forget to breathe.

ASPECTS

Builds power and motor skill control into the whole of the lower body. See Squat Jumps.

RELATED MOVEMENTS

Scissor Jumps: At mid position, switch leg position (front to back, back to front). This must be done lightning fast in order to land in the correct position. Attainment of maximum height is required.

Double Scissor Jumps: For those who think they are too cool for school: Mid position; a complete cycle of the legs (front to back, back to front, and vice versa) is required curriculum.

Leg Press

Top position — This movement lends itself to the smoothing out of jerky transition phases.

Bottom position — Consider this: Resistance responds to the inward thrusts of your energy; it creates its own energy that needs to be tended to by concentration.

MOVEMENT

Resistance is pressed to near extension at top position. A slow negative phase is countered at the bottom position by an authoritative transition into the positive phase. Be careful not to bounce the weight as the knees draw close to the chest.

ABSTRACTS

Like a stream, strive for flowing movement and a steady tempo. This movement lends itself to smoothing out jerky, novice-like transition phases.

ASPECTS

Trains more of the frontal thigh and less of the gluteal region. An excellent pre-fatiguing and finishing movement.

RELATED MOVEMENTS

Diagonal Leg Press: This is pictured. Available at most facilities and is well worth exploration.

Other Related Movements: Vertical Leg Press, Nautilus Leg Press, and Horizontal Leg Press.

Lunges

Bottom position of a Touch 'n Go Lunge. A world of creative, highly effective variations of this movement lies unknown to the common strength trainer.

MOVEMENT

Description for Touch 'n Go Lunges: Start as in Back Squats. Like a fencer, lunge forward onto one leg, landing softly and on a flat foot. Top of the thigh is parallel to the ground. Now explode back to the start position.

ABSTRACTS

An excellent athletic movement in which increased poundage is applied in a safe fashion. Upper body is erect and proud. Maintain sharp, crisp, and clean movements. Overload can be applied by length of stride, poundage increases, speed of return phase, and increased tempo (leg exchange/recovery ratio).

ASPECTS

Splendid movement that develops strength, power, and agility in the buttocks, frontal and rear thighs, and rear calf.

RELATED MOVEMENTS

Strength Lunges: Instead of explosively returning back to start position, weight the extended (lunging) leg. Repeat by bringing forward the opposite leg. An uncrowded distance is needed for these. More weight is used in this variant.

Static Lunges: Lunging leg remains forward. A weighting and unweighting of the leg is then performed. Each leg is exercised independently.

Side Lunges: Can be performed "statically" or "dynamically" as in Touch 'n Go Lunges. Lead leg is placed, or lunged, to the side of start position, respectively.

Step-Ups: These are Touch 'n Go Lunges done onto a box or surface. The height of the lunging surface can be progressively increased, yielding another form of overload.

GP Squats

Bottom position, GP Squat. Derived from a ballet movement. I borrowed that art's demand for rigidity of form, extracted its call for flowing texture, and applied it all to a pair of pre-fatigued thighs. The result? Do them, then you tell me.

MOVEMENT

Place feet wide and to the side. Toes point outward. Heels are raised, strong contraction occurs in the calf. Press knees out to the side. Upper torso and the head are pulled up, and all rigidity of the vertical, flat back is maintained. Body is balanced at arm's length by one hand. Action sequence is a methodical and extremely slow up-and-down motion. Go very deep.

ABSTRACTS

I took this from the ballet movement, the Grand Plie (thus the name). It is usually performed as the second in a superset. A very cerebral exercise. Fantastic for discovering the finer side to strength, like realizing just what is meant by "Lift from the glutes." All lifting faculties are called upon. Relaxation is the key to effective strength.

ASPECTS

Primary emphasis falls upon the gluteal region. Numerous stabilization and assistive work is done by the midsection musculature and the calf muscles.

RELATED MOVEMENTS

Weighted GPs: With the free hand, grasp a dumbbell.

Ski Stances: Remain statically in bottom position. The more common variant is done against the wall. The reader of this book will have none of that.

Leg Curls

The Ilg Variant. Such positioning greatly enhances the ability to pre-contract and cancel out unnecessary muscles which clot absolute form.

MOVEMENT

Lie face-down on a Lying Leg Curl machine with heels placed against the foot bar. Pre-contract the buttock musculature, then curl the heels toward the same area. Negative phase is the lowering action from top position.

ABSTRACTS

Most trainers will yell at you: "Keep your hips down!" This never helped me. I say this: "Pre-contract the buttocks and lift your abdominals off the vinyl." Immediately, this contraction isolates the buttocks and hip muscles from assisting the curling motion. The result: A purer, more effectual contraction of the rear thigh.

ASPECTS

Primarily a rear thigh strengthening movement. Secondary emphasis goes to calf musculature.

RELATED MOVEMENTS

Standing and Seated Leg Curls: Done on apparatuses of the same name.

Partner-Assisted Leg Curls: For those without access to a machine, a partner can take the akinetic place of a weight stack and give resistance to both phases of the lift.

Stiff Leg Deadlifts

Nearing bottom position — Lower back problems are nonexistent to the practitioneer of this movement.

MOVEMENT

Start standing upright with a barbell held at arm's length. Bend forward at the waist, allowing the dead weight of the barbell to follow a natural path downward. Head is kept pulled up, eyes look forward, never downward. Maintain the integrity of the flat back (note photo) until the flatness becomes rounded. Return.

ABSTRACTS

This exercise is an affair with performance-enhancing postural awareness. Like affairs, much flirtation is needed. Knees are never bent, and the indispensable "flat lower back" is paramount to proper execution. Lower back problems are non-existent to the practitioner of this movement.

ASPECTS

A flexibility and strengthening effect is realized almost immediately. Stresses the lumbar muscles of the lower back, and elongates in a very safe, progressive manner the hamstrings of the leg.

RELATED MOVEMENTS

Good Mornings: Identical philosophy; the exception is the bar placement which is carried as in Back Squats.

Seated Good Mornings: Need more really be said?

Calf Raises

Top position — Sometimes people snicker and tell me I have small calves. My reply? "So do thoroughbred race horses."

MOVEMENT

Contingent upon apparatus. Commonality: Achieve strong contraction point by raising the heels as high as possible. The negative (lowering here) phase should be carried as deep (low) as possible.

ABSTRACTS

An important ankle-joint-strengthening movement for all athletes. Slow tempo. Hold the top position to feel the essence of calf work. Don't shy away from heavy resistance; the calf complex is a formidable one.

ASPECTS

Trains the gastrocnemius and soleus (rear calf) musculature, and an attentive negative phase stresses and lengthens the achilles tendon area, and the tibialis anterior region (frontal calf musculature).

RELATED MOVEMENTS

(Pictured is the Seated Calf Raise.)

Standing Calf Raise: Done on a variety of machines, from Nautilus to a barbell positioned across the upper back.

Donkey Calf Raise: A superb variant. Tools needed: One or preferably more grossly overweight friends. Stand on a staircase like in the bottom position of a Stiff Leg Deadlift, except hands are placed on a step, and the heels float off the edge of a lower stair. Place tools on your flat back. Now raise and lower the heels.

Midsection

Abdominal Crunches

Top position — A misunderstood exercise. Tension is everything.

MOVEMENT

Supine. Upper leg bones perpendicular to the earth, knees at a right angle. Toes up. Press the lower back to the ground, curl the upper torso toward the knees. Attain a mental and physical peak contraction in the abdominals, pause, then slowly force the abdominals to be the "brake" that lets the upper torso float back down to start position.

ABSTRACTS

A largely misunderstood exercise. If you can do a lot of repetitions, you are missing the exercise. A very cerebral exercise demanding much concentration. Tension is everything; opposing contractile forces in the midsection are a must. Lower back never leaves its connection to the earth.

ASPECTS

Trains the frontal abdominal muscles and offers a strong center for a wide application to many athletic movements. A classic.

RELATED MOVEMENTS

Twist Crunches: In the top position, bring the right elbow across the body's midline to touch the left knee or calf. Return to start position, alternate, repeat.

Reach-Thru's: A most enjoyable abdominal outing. My favorite. Supine: Heels are kept earthbound, shoulder-width, and near the buttocks. Lower back pressed flat, elbows are flared out to the sides, hands float above chest. From here, the hands "Reach-Thru" the legs, attempting to touch the nearest wall. Return to start. Maintain good tempo.

Holding Reach-Thru's: As the top position is attained in the standard Reach-Thru, statically hold the peak contraction point. Usually held for a five count.

Inversion Crunches: An advanced technique which requires countering the dynamics of being upside down and performing a crunching type of movement. A training partner acts as a brace to limit swing. All the above techniques are applicable.

Russian Twists

Mid position — An advanced movement which develops tremendous midsection power.

MOVEMENT

Start as pictured. Now, keeping a seat of tremendous tensile strength in the abdominals, lower the extended arms first to one side, then the other. Progressive resistance is achieved by grasping barbell plates.

ABSTRACTS

An advanced exercise that develops tremendous midsection power. Caution is advised; remember that training must be a constructive stress. Proceed patiently.

ASPECTS

Much force is centralized on and must be countered by the frontal abdominals, the obliques, and the serratus musculature. Tensile strength is developed in the lumbar region of the back, while the upper torso muscle must stabilize the arm swing.

RELATED MOVEMENTS

Seated Twisting: A more genteel alternative in the same genus. Using a bar, broomstick to a weighted Olympic barbell, assume a seated position with the bar placed across the upper back. Creating from the abdominals, swing the bar side to side. Midsection checks, counters the transitions. Keep looking forward.

Leg Raises

Top position — A particularly excellent movement which teaches the concept of working from one's center.

MOVEMENT

Begin by contracting mentally the abdominals. Leg position: Extended, but with a slight bend at the knee. Toes point away. Positive phase: The angle between torso and legs decreases. Negative phase: Angle between torso and legs increases.

ABSTRACTS

A particularly excellent movement teaching the athlete to "work from the center." Done slowly with an emphasis on elegance. Can be done on a variety of apparatuses.

ASPECTS

Stresses the abdominal wall from the advantageous perspective of increased leverage provided by leg extension.

RELATED MOVEMENTS

Suspended Variant (pictured): Can be done lying down, hanging from a chinning bar, and even "seated" (using the arms to support upper torso on a dipping bar).

Three-Way Leg Raises: Maintaining good control, "shoot" the legs off to one side, then the other.

Throw-Downs: An advanced movement. A training partner stands near and "throws" your legs downward during the negative phase as you attempt to counter the force.

"Ab Wheel"

Bottom position — The incredible contractions inherent to this movement exceed all other attempts at abdominal training.

MOVEMENT

Using the apparatus, begin with it at arm's length directly below the chest. Tighten buttock muscles. Consciously tense the abdominals. Working now from this "centrality" principle, roll the "wheel" out from you. Return.

ABSTRACTS

Learn this advanced exercise, and you've learned just about every modern athletic performance training principle there is.

ASPECTS

Primary motion is the responsibility of the abdominal wall, although the assistive effect required is nearly the entire body.

RELATED MOVEMENTS

Self-Assistive "Ab Wheels": Brace your heels up against the bottom of a chair or the likeness thereof. Now perform the movement, using the benefits of a "Leg Curl" motion.

Lower Back Work

See Stiff Leg Deadlifts Description.

Upper Body

Pullups

Left: Top position — Pullups widen the back and promote an aesthetic "V" shape. *Right:* A variant, the "V" Handle Pullup. The beauty of the Pullup lies in its diversity.

MOVEMENT

Grip a pullup bar, palms facing out and placed a bit wider than shoulder width. Knees are bent at ninety degrees. Raise yourself until arms are at least parallel to the earth, preferably higher. Lower to bottom position. Repeat. Note: To maximize muscular development and to limit elbow joint stress, the majority of pullup training should be done by keeping the elbows slightly flexed in the bottom position.

ABSTRACTS

A glorious movement that never gets any easier but results in preternatural athletic gains. The beauty of this movement lies in its diversified ability to validate strength gains from a wide range of angles and motions. Grip changes, range of movement versatility, and "prop" integration all contribute to the importance of this lift. From a general appearance perspective, Pullups widen the back and promote an aesthetic "V" shape.

ASPECTS

A very pure latissimus dorsi movement, albeit central and deeper back musculature is emphasized as well.

RELATED MOVEMENTS

Behind-the-Neck Pullups: Instead of pulling the chest toward the bar, top position is attained by touching the upper back to the bar.

V-Handle Pullups: As pictured. A "V" handle prop is needed, although a towel might suffice.

Weighted Pullups: A dipping belt or an equivalent strap hold a dumbbell between the legs to increase overload.

One-Arm Pullups: Good for parties, but have little athletic transfer practicality. Practicing the movement results in a great degree of elbow joint trauma.

Pulldowns

Bottom position — Ilg shows how to flush the back
with strength-building sensations by adhering to
rhythmic form.

MOVEMENT

Done on a Pulldown machine. Take a slightly wider than shoulder width grip on the bar. Upper torso should lean away from the machine. Pull the bar downward (this is the positive phase) to the bottom position which is just below the chin. Overexaggerate bringing the chest out "to meet the bar." Maintain a flat back; and initiate negative phase by controlling the bar back to top position.

ABSTRACTS

A distant second to Pullups, but offers good training. A variety of bars and grips presents ample opportunity for fresh stimulation. Envision pulling the elbows so close together in the bottom position that they touch.

ASPECTS

A similar, although less stimulative effect, as in Pullups.

RELATED MOVEMENTS

Behind-the-Neck Pulldowns: As the name suggests. Pull the bar to upper back for a completed repetition.

Pulldown Prop Work: A wide spectrum of handles and other more esoteric attachments can be parlayed into a better degree of sport-specific strength.

2-Way Ilgs

Left: First phase, top position — Feel the flow of good form. *Right:* Second phase, nearing top position — The variations are numerous and guarantee a good workout.

MOVEMENT

Divided into two distinct phases: First phase is a Bent Over Row. Feet are placed at shoulder width, knees bent; a flat back is parallel to the earth. Pull the bar from arm's length toward the chest area. Get the contraction. Begin the negative phase back to start. Repeat.

The second phase is a Barbell Shrug. Immediately after MMF is reached in the first phase, stand erect and in good posture. With the bar at arm's length, keep the elbows straight and raise the shoulder girdle up as far as possible.

ABSTRACTS

A most encompassing method to train the back. When selecting poundages for the Set and Repetition schemes, use the first phase to establish your resistance. The second phase is one of quick tempo and higher repetitions. It is easy to veer from clear breathing during this exercise, so stay alert to good form. Feel the flow of good form.

ASPECTS

Trains the latissimus dorsi, trapezius, erector spinae, rhomboideus, teres complex, posterior deltoid, with strong reliance upon assistive and synergistic musculature for stabilization and control purposes.

RELATED MOVEMENTS

Variations are numerous and guarantee a good workout. Beginners might do One-Arm Dumbbell Rows for the first phase, and advanced weightlifters would have fun substituting Power or Hang Cleans or High Pulls in lieu of Bent Over Rows.

PowerCleans

Left: The hip extension phase. *Center:* Entering the "catch" phase. Note the velocity of the bar . . . no room for timidity here! *Right:* Top position — I say this: Practice, visualize, practice some more.

MOVEMENT

The Set-Up: Stand over a weighted barbell. Bend at the knees and grasp the bar at shoulder width. Set hips low, shins near the bar, and back is flat. Look ahead, not down. Arms are extended.

Phase One, The Sl . . . ow Pull: From the set-up position, pull the bar off the floor (DO NOT JERK THE BAR UP), then, without pause:

Phase Two, The Hip Extension or "Jump": As the bar slowly passes the knees, explosively pull the bar toward the chest. At mid-thigh level, simultaneously do this: Shrug the shoulders and get the elbows up toward the ceiling. Hips will come forward (extension) and the feet should leave the floor. And . . .

Phase Three, The Catch: Do not interfere with the velocity that your shrug and hip extension have given the barbell. Let the barbell reach its maximum height, then quickly move under the bar and "catch" it on the upper chest.

Repeat by reversing the movements with a pause at mid-thigh, then to the floor. Go again.

ABSTRACTS

PowerClean is the most phenomenal lift ever invented. It borders on the metaphysical. All I can say is this: Practice, visualize, practice some more.

ASPECTS

Trains all the muscular components as in 2-Way Ilgs, but does so in a far more explosive (powerful) manner. Thus, the more physiological factors are stressed, manifesting in a wider appeal to athletic performance. A very psychologically demanding movement.

RELATED MOVEMENTS

Hang Cleans: Start position is with the barbell held at arm's length, near mid-thigh. Now go to Phase Two of the PowerClean. Keep the back flat! Return to start position.

High Pulls: A lift that deserves far more attention than it is currently receiving. Start and pull as in Hang Cleans, but do not "catch" the bar; simply pull it toward the chin, then lower back to start. Rapid tempo with much blast on the positive phase is needed.

Seated Rows

Start position — Strive for body unity.

Top position — Do away with superfluous exertion.

MOVEMENT

Done off a lower pulley cable. Start position needs a flat back, knees bent as pictured, and a stretching sensation in the central back. Begin with a positive phase: As the handle is pulled toward you, push the chest outward and slide into a flat, upright back position. This creates a far better contraction point for the top position. Negative phase is done with elegance and precise control.

ABSTRACTS

Make this movement immaculate. Strive for body unity in the pull; reach inward for an electric lowering phase which contains all stored muscle tension . . . do away with superfluous exertion.

RELATED MOVEMENTS

Variants include a high pulley cable, various handles, various grips, and, of course, various techniques and creativity.

Full Deadlift

The lift phase of the Full Deadlift.

Living for the moment: In the lockout phase of the Full Deadlift. At advanced levels, "Deads" transcend conventional training effort and persuade the lifter to stare directly into the splintering of his own limitations.

MOVEMENT

Start as in PowerCleans. The exercise reaches top position as the body stands erect with shoulders drawn back.

ABSTRACTS

One of the three Powerlifts, known for its full-body involvement. Much virtue lies within this simple movement. I encourage each reader to integrate this lift into his/her training at some point. At advanced levels, "Deads" transcend conventional training effort and persuade the lifter to stare directly at the splintering of his/her own limitations.

ASPECTS

Like all Powerlifts, this is a multi-joint movement. The biomechanics of the lift reveal emphasis on:

The Liftoff: Gluteal (buttock), quadricep, and hamstring musculature for knee and hip extension.

The Midway Pull: Emphasis stays on the gluteals and quadriceps for knee and hip extension, but is now assisted by the trapezius (upper back) for vertebral extension.

The Lockout: A coordinated blending of knee, hip, and vertebral extension. The erector spinae muscles of the lower back are quite important here for complete lumbar extension to achieve top position.

RELATED MOVEMENTS

There are none save for the Top Deadlift, which simply starts with the bar situated near knee height. Blocks can be used to achieve this starting point.

Dips

Left: Start/Bottom position — What Squats are to the lower body, Dips are to the upper body. *Right:* Top position — Accept the fact that Dips are difficult . . . the best things for you always are . . . then get on with them, for improvement comes quickly.

L.C.M. (Lateral Chest Movements)

Left: Bottom position — One of the numerous variants under the L.C.M. category.
Right: Top position — Flye movements are the quintessence of concentration.

MOVEMENT

Dumbbell Flat Flyes described: Lie supine on a flat bench. Spine is pressed against bench's surface; don't arch from that connection. Two dumbbells are grasped overhead. Elbows are bent slightly — maybe ten degrees. From this point on, DO NOT CHANGE THAT ANGLE — articulation will spring from the shoulder joint, not the elbow. From this top position, a negative phase initiates a lowering of the bells to the side, done in smooth, semicircular motion. The range of this descent is determined by one's flexibility. A positive phase rushes the bells back to top position.

ABSTRACTS

I've created a category of lateral chest maneuvers labeled L.C.M. So many beautiful variations exist, I did not wish to limit your choices. The above description can be conceptually applied to all the related movements found below. Flye movements are the quintessence of concentration in the gym. Every inch must be felt, less the tension leave and the training effect diminish.

ASPECTS

Stresses the pectoralis musculature, both in the sternal and clavicular regions.

RELATED MOVEMENTS

Dumbbell Incline Flyes: Find an incline bench, grab a light pair of bells, and experiment using the above movement description. This emphasizes the upper chest.

Dumbbell Decline Flyes: Same as Dumbbell Incline or Flat Flyes, but done in a decline bench. Stresses the lower chest.

Cable Flyes: All the above descriptions can be transferred into cable exercises using both low and high pulleys.

Pec-Dec Flyes: Includes Nautilus and all the other machine versions available. Remember your flowing negative/positive rhythm, and feel every inch.

Bench Press

Left: Bottom position — "The Bench", as it is affectionately called, is another one of the three powerlifts. *Right:* Top position — An overrated exercise. Be satisfied with less poundage, but more composure in elegant technique. Your joints will thank you.

MOVEMENT

Supine on a flat bench. Top position is with a barbell over the chest at arm's extension. Grip: Shoulder width. Negative phase starts as the bar is lowered to mid-chest area. Positive phase back to top.

ABSTRACTS

In my opinion, this is a grossly overrated and overpopularized lift. Maybe that's because I continually have to rehabilitate torn shoulders which are the by-products of poor technique on this exercise. A lot (too much?) of the stress is placed on the shoulder during the motion, so be alert. No lower back arching, please. Be satisfied with less poundage but more composure in elegant technique. Your joints will thank you.

ASPECTS

Trains the pectoralis complex, and the anterior deltoid. Secondary action calls for the tricep group.

RELATED MOVEMENTS

Decline and Incline Bench Press: Same philosophy, different benches.

Dumbbell Bench Press: Same philosophy, different tools. A better choice for athletes, I think, because it brings into play a greater demand of neuromuscular and motor skill control factors.

Repetition Jerks

Left: Start of the Repetition Jerk — A speed-strength movement. One of my favorites for all types of athletes. *Right:* Top position — Remember, no pressing allowed!

A student once told me that she began seeing God at rep 16 . . .

MOVEMENT

Begin in the top position of the PowerClean. Dip down by slightly bending the knees. Store tension in the buttocks and thighs at this point. Now, very rapidly using that stored hip and leg power, jerk the bar directly overhead. This is a speed (power) movement; therefore, do not press the bar at all. The bar attains the top position as a simple manifestation of lower body explosion. Now, begin a slow negative phase back to start position.

ABSTRACTS

A poorly named but phenomenal strength and power movement. I cannot overstress the value of realizing the power stored in the lower body. Notice how the bar literally vaults off the chest toward the ceiling on a good rep. When this happens, you have begun to understand true power.

ASPECTS

A speed-strength developer for the entire deltoid (shoulder) complex.

RELATED MOVEMENTS

Power Snatch: Start with bar resting on mid-thigh. In one extremely fast movement, simultaneously shrug the bar upward and jump under it as it reaches its apex, catching the bar at arm's length. Remember — no pressing allowed. A wide grip is needed.

Seated Press

Left: Start position — A well-orchestrated linkage of reps, when done in quick tempo, is a key to optimal strength-training results. *Right:* Top position — Shoulder work provides an excellent opportunity to work on this.

MOVEMENT

Done seated. Bar placement as in top position of the PowerClean, palms facing outward. Positive phase: Press the weight directly overhead, not forward. Negative phase: Lower the weight to start (bottom) position.

ABSTRACTS

Strengthens the shoulder group to an unmatched degree. Grip width may vary for stimulation of fresh muscle fibers. Keep a flat back, one centered precisely over the hips. Make a clean, sprightly positive, and a shoulder-burning, slow negative. The use of a weight belt comes recommended.

ASPECTS

Targets the shoulders in direct fashion. Peripheral benefits include an "opening" or freeing of the scapular region of the back in order to stabilize the weight in the top position.

RELATED MOVEMENTS

(Barbell Seated Press pictured.)

Dumbbell Seated Press: When done with dumbbells, a greater call for balance is needed. Practice with light dumbbells initially. Dumbbells necessitate a more semicircular fluidity than machine or barbell work.

Press-Behind-Neck: Bottom position is the back of the neck. This variation switches stimulation to the middle section of the shoulder (medial deltoid).

Machine Press: Self-explanatory. A well-orchestrated linkage of reps done with quick tempo; is a key to optimal strength-training results. Shoulder work provides an excellent opportunity to work on this.

Side Lateral Raises

Left: Bottom position — A certain degree of shoulder-searing charm lies within its execution. *Right:* Top position — Contrary to popular belief, top position does not need to be done to an overhead position. In fact, doing so can be dangerous.

MOVEMENT

Stand holding two dumbbells at mid-thigh. Elbows are flexed at about fifteen degrees. Back is flat. Knees are slightly bent. Head is up. Shoulder girdle is relaxed. In a good positive phase form, raise the bells high to your sides, in simpatico. Top position, contrary to popular belief, needs not to be overhead, but only until the upper arm bone breaks parallel to the floor (any movement beyond this creates an unnatural torque within the shoulder joint, and when progressive resistance is applied, the joint danger outweighs any effects that could be gained). The negative phase should be at least half as slow as the positive, and is returned to bottom position.

ABSTRACTS

This is a worthwhile lift to practice a lot. Many energy pathways can be discovered along the way. A certain degree of shoulder-searing charm lies within its execution. High reps are good here. Slow that negative phase, and don't forget to breathe!

ASPECTS

A direct deltoid (shoulder) movement that cancels out the majority of tricep influence common to most rear-arm exercises.

RELATED MOVEMENTS

Machine Side Lateral Raises: I do not like most machines available for this movement. By only allowing one linear plane to accommodate everyone's biomechanics, I've found that most machines create micro-traumas upon the complexities of shoulder after training on them for a while. This "one-size-fits-all" approach seems a risky one to me.

Bent Over Side Laterals: Can be done seated or standing. Bend over and allow the bells to hang down, keeping them bent. Raise them to the sides until they pass the torso-line of your back. Lower (negative phase) to bottom position. Variant: Face in toward the upright of an incline bench. Arms with bells hang at your side. Perform the movement from here. These are called Prone Incline Laterals.

Front Lateral Raises: Do these; you'll like them. Can be done with dumbbells or a barbell. Instead of performing the positive and negatives to the sides, the movement is done to the front of you.

Lying Triceps Extension

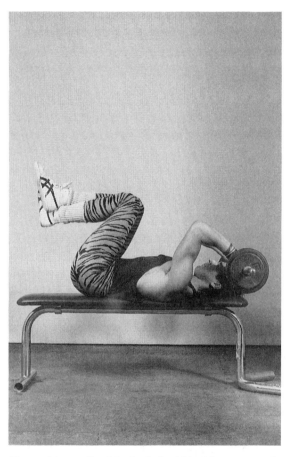

Top position — Don't be fooled; within this movement's simplicity and purity is great complexity. Ten years, and I'm still learning the inner details of this movement.

MOVEMENT

Supine. Hold a barbell at arm's length, palms away from you. Grip width can vary but should be shoulder width or narrower. Upper arm bone remains fixed; this is an elbow, not a shoulder, movement. From this top position, perform a slower than usual negative phase until the bar touches the hairline of your head. Smooth transition. Explode your positive phase up to top position. Repeat.

ABSTRACTS

Have your body listen for the details of this movement. Ten years, and I'm still learning it. The simplicity and purity of this exercise offer great rewards. Be aware of the lower back; the tendency is to arch. Feet up in the air will keep such nonsense in check. A "false" grip is suggested here (thumbs on the same side of the bar as the fingers).

ASPECTS

A very strict triceps brachii motion. Some stabilization occurs in the chest and shoulder areas.

RELATED MOVEMENTS

Standing Triceps Extension: In archaic gym lexicon, the French Press. No big differences in technique, just perform standing with the upper arm bone striving to be perpendicular. This variation can be done off a lower pulley on a cable machine, which seems to work better because of more continuous tension placed upon the muscle.

Dumbbell Tricep Extension: Each of the above can be done employing dumbbells in lieu of a barbell.

Dumbbell Kickbacks

Left: Start position — Variations include a palm up, palm down, and rotating palm versions. *Right:* Top position — A particularly valuable movement for skiers.

MOVEMENT

Start position as pictured. Upper arm is parallel to the floor; the elbow joint forms a right angle. The palm faces toward the body, and the hand grasps a light dumbbell. Positive phase: Straighten the lower arm backward as far as possible. Lower back to bottom position using good negative form.

ABSTRACTS

In the *Complete Weight Training Book* (World Publications), my friend Bill Reynolds calls this exercise a developer of "maximum contractile power" for the triceps. Particularly valuable for skiers.

ASPECTS

Isolates the triceps brachii while requiring a precise peak contraction in the top position.

RELATED MOVEMENTS

Variations include a palm up, palm down, and rotating palm versions. Also, the upper arm can be situated out to the side; sometimes this assists in achieving a more forceful positive phase.

2-Bench Triceps

Bottom position — A great movement for those who aspire to "Dips" and for advanced athletes to "polish off" a tricep workout.

MOVEMENT

Body is suspended between two benches; palms facing backward on one bench, calves resting upon the surface of the other. Begin with a negative phase, lowering from the elbows so as to attempt touching the buttocks to the floor. Now, in positive phase explosiveness, push back to top position.

ABSTRACTS

An underestimated movement. Great for "polishing off" the triceps or for beginning lifters on their way to performing Dips. Keep the back flat, and remember — "There are reps in breath."

ASPECTS

A triceps brachii endurance builder that relies upon the shoulder for help.

RELATED MOVEMENTS

Partner 2-Bench's: Have a training partner push down on your upper back for added resistance on both phases.

Self-Assisted 2-Bench's: For beginners learning the movement or for continuing standard form past MMF: Place one foot on the floor (the other remains on the "leg" bench), and "feed" off of it to get up to top position as the positive becomes impossible to perform.

Pressdowns

Bottom position — This triceps brachii movement has direct positive implications for shoulder joint health by way of strengthening the capsular ligament.

MOVEMENT

Face the machine. Grip the handle with palms facing down. Start (top) position is with the lower arm bones just past parallel to the floor. Keep elbows "pressured" against your sides. Positive phase down from here to complete arm extension. Feel the triceps contract statically in this bottom position. Now, allow that contraction to "brake" the handle as it rises back to top position.

ABSTRACTS

A generous movement for the back of the arms. Fantastic construction of a strength foundation for a pair of athletic arms. Rigidity to abdominal wall please. Stay "pulled up" and limit any surplus body activity. Pressdowns can be done off a cable machine (high pulley), or a lat pulldown machine.

ASPECTS

Direct triceps brachii movement (the majority of the contraction occurring in the long head), which has positive implications for shoulder joint health (via capsular ligament strengthening effect).

RELATED MOVEMENTS

Undergrip Pressdowns: Instead of the above described common overgrip, take a palms-up grip and proceed with the movement. More emphasis will now fall upon the medial and short heads of the triceps brachii.

Rope Pressdowns: The "thinking man's" alternative. Using rope permits greater freedom to the bottom position, allowing the athlete to "splay" the ends outward.

Barbell Curl

Mid position — Let your curls become a meditative affair. Rivet your energies to the feel, to the dance of the lift. Curl from within, and take note of the sensations.

MOVEMENT

Stand with the weight at arm's length, elbows slightly bent and close to the sides of the body. Grip: Shoulder width or narrower. Positive phase: Curl the weight upward by flexion of the elbow joint. Attain a strong contraction point up top by elevating both upper arms slightly. Negative phase: Lower the weight downward to bottom position.

ABSTRACTS

Keep back flat; say "no" to the common tendency to swing the weight during positive phases then just letting the bar drop back to bottom position. This is foolish behavior and has no place in an athlete's training. Let your curls become as all of training — a meditative affair. Rivet your energies to the feel, to the dance of the lift. Curl from within, and take note of the sensations.

ASPECTS

A basic movement soliciting action from the bicep brachii, the brachialis (an upper arm muscle), and the brachioradialis (an upper and lower arm muscle).

RELATED MOVEMENTS

Dumbbell Curl: Done by using two dumbbells in place of a barbell.

Apparatus Curls: Runs the spectrum from an "ancient" Scott or Preacher Curl Bench, to Nautilus things, and finally to wonderments like the Tygr Electronically Resistive Eccentric/Concentric Programmable Incline Machine.

Seated Alternating Dumbbell Curl

Left: Start position — Note the unconventional starting point for the upper arm. This pre-contraction of the triceps (rear upper arm muscle) may provide the biceps with a stretch reflex condition, resulting in a far greater overload for the biceps. *Right:* Top position — A nemesis lift for the faineant.

MOVEMENT

Take a seat. Feet may be elevated; this insures minimal hip and lower back involvement. An incline bench (the angle of the upright may be varied) is suggested. Important starting notation: Arms must parallel the angle of your bench's upright. Palms face each other beneath your bench. The dumbbells should be of light to moderate weight. One arm at a time; from the "dead spot" start position, a slower than usual positive phase curls the weight upward with little upper arm sway. As the bell rises, initiate wrist supination; turn the palm upward. By the top position (see photo), this twist should be at its greatest. Now begin a negative phase back to bottom position. Do other arm. Repeat.

ABSTRACTS

A nemesis lift for the faineant. You'll find the intermingling speeds of the downward, upward, and rotational pulsations overwhelming for the biceps of the arm. A superb exercise that has all the requisites of a classic strength-training movement. It demands concentration, rhythm, effectual breathing, high contractile and elasticity points, and neuromuscular centering.

ASPECTS

A cataclysmic event for the flexors of the elbow. An unequalled movement for the biceps brachii, brachialis, brachioradialis.

RELATED MOVEMENTS

Orthodox Style: At start position, arms hand directly downward. Proceed with the movement described above.

Reverse Wrist Curl

Midway through the forearm torching, Reverse Wrist
Curl. Train through the burn, not to it.

MOVEMENT

Grip a light barbell in the manner pictured above. Palms are down. The underside of the forearm should remain in constant contact with the bench's surface. Hands are suspended in air. Positive phase: Bend at the wrist in an upward motion. Lower to perform the negative phase.

ABSTRACTS

A torcher. Keep a flat back. Breathe. Train through the burn, not to it. At latter stages of the set, a little inflection from perfect form might net a few more reps. Go for it.

ASPECTS

A pronounced strengthening effect occurs in the wrist joint due to a balancing of often stressed wrist flexor muscles by isolating the extensor musculature of the wrist.

RELATED MOVEMENTS

Dumbbell Variant: Same exercise but use two or one dumbbell(s) in substitution for a barbell.

Finger Curls: Stand upright. The tips of your fingers grasp the indented edge of a suitable barbell plate. Keep a slight flex at the elbow. Curl your fingers from near extension toward the base of your palm. Go slowly and study. This is a superb ligament and tendon strengthener.

Wrist Curl

Mid position — You might find yourself asking this post-Wrist Curl set question: How can such a small muscle hurt so much? The answer: Good question.

MOVEMENT

Similar start position as in Reverse Wrist Curls. Assume the more common "undergrip" on a moderate to heavy barbell. Positive phase is the curling (upward bending) motion of the wrist. Negative phase is the lowering. Bottom position is not attained until the barbell is rolled all the way down to the first joint of the fingers. Repeat.

ABSTRACTS

I exclude a lot of direct forearm work in my training approach for outdoor athletes. I've found that the fatigue/recovery ratio is long enough to warrant concern for overtraining the musculature. A wiser forearm training approach might be to use these indoor exercises as a means to strengthen the ligamentous structure of the wrist, then allowing sport-specific activities (say buildering or bouldering to improve the grip-strength potential of the technical rock climber) to increase specifically needed strengths. Additionally, realize that the constant gripping and ungripping of barbells, etc., in the gym account for a significant training effect for the forearms.

ASPECTS

Perhaps the most valuable aspect of forearm training in a gym-type environment is from a joint health perspective. By training in balanced manner, the flexors and the extensors (as is accomplished via Wrist Curls and Reverse Wrist Curls, respectively), the overall connective strength of the wrist joint is assured.

RELATED MOVEMENTS

Wrist Rollers: This is basically a bar (or dowel) with a cord through the middle of its length. At the free end of the cord is the resistance. The exercise is one of winding up the cord, then back down.

Tennis Ball Squeezes, and Etc.: The only dilemma here is one of progressive resistance. You can't get stronger unless the musculature is forced to adapt to a heavier workload. That is the inherent flaw to most forearm training gadgets.

Flexibility is beauty. Like certain forms of music, one must listen closely in order to extract the essences of what the sound is telling you.

Flexibility Movements

Model: Joyce Rossiter. All photographs by Legere Photography, Ilg archives.

Flexibility means joints that are free and open. This takes time, but that's okay, because flexibility is sensitivity. And sensitivity can never be rushed.

Flexibility is a meditative type of thing. Mimic the movements you see here, but do so with softness. The ballerina shown here has been doing these types of stretches for many years. So, unless you are a ballerina who has been doing movements like these for many years, mimic the motion and see into the movements your own ability.

Flexibility is a form of surrender. Like the fragrances of nature, flexibility comes without intention. Do your stretching in a warm place filled with delicate energy; a few quiet moments are all that is needed.

Flexibility is a supple response to an unclouded mind. The movements: Crisp and done cleanly without so much as thought itself to disturb your peace of self. As your muscles elongate, so, too, will your sense of inner calm lengthen.

Flexibility is breath. As you ease into your stretches, your breath will want to exhale the sweet daggers of "pain" which arise from within. Let it. While holding the stretch, be sure to breathe. Deeply. (Fifteen breaths to a stretch will change any troubling emotion into a more positive thought which can then be acted upon.) Remember this the next time life tries to hurry you past your natural way.

Flexibility is progressive. With the birth pangs of increased joint range come a new sense of self. It may seem uncompact, even disheveled. This is a side of you that is escaping into outside energies. Keep stretching and explore.

Flexibility is not logical. Growing flexible means melting walls of mental constructs. Set your emotions aside. Training for suppleness means living a world of intellectual anarchy. Think about that. Realize what the phrase "sense of self" really means.

Flexibility is joyfulness. Initiate and share flexibility sessions with a friend. This is great fun. Creativity flows and the humor is doubled. Be careful to move gingerly and in natural body lines.

Flexibility is harmony. Stretching is related to flexibility only as one of many tools. Others may be: Staying relaxed during every day; maximizing that happy part of you; releasing into youthful exuberance just for fun; being kind and open-hearted; capitalizing on your ability to trust life.

Flexibility is the great extractor. Exercise puts stress into musculature. Flexibility removes it. Movement becomes pure again. So free! So light! So open! All is well because flexibility rehabilitates self- and society-induced restraints which injure us in ways we may not even recognize.

Flexibility is reinvigorating. It is joint health. It is calmness. It is body awareness. It is meditation. It is religion. It is the moonlight in your lap. Have fun.

Appendices:
Some Extra Stuff

Appendix A:
Sports Injuries:
Some Questions for
Dr. Mark Robinson

In December 1987, I shared a podium with Dr. Mark Robinson during a featured "Training for Climbing" presentation at the annual meeting of the American Alpine Club. Dr. Robinson is a board-certified orthopaedic surgeon practicing in Ventura, California. Over the years, he has participated extensively in rock climbing, mountaineering, hiking, bicycling, mountain cycling, running, swimming, and surfing. His practice includes a large number of sports injuries, and he has a keen interest in injuries arising from noncompetitive outdoor sports.

In preparing this second edition, I asked Dr. Robinson to respond to questions I had in my files from clients and readers. Although these queries have come from athletes around the globe, their answers hit a very small place — the individual performer.

"I'm almost always in pain to some degree; how can I tell how serious it is?"
The real question is whether what you feel is *pain* or not. The sore feeling that comes after a workout is not necessarily bad or even pain. The sensation of a pump after a maximal effort isn't either. These are good sensations, and give you clues about the quality of effort. Delayed soreness is bad and represents muscle

damage. Unpleasant sensations accompanied by swelling, tenderness, or other such signs indicate local tissue damage. These sensations are indeed painful and tell you to slow down or stop to allow healing. Pain which produces a limp or makes you feel you aren't enjoying the activity probably also indicates too much use.

"What type of injuries require heat, and which require cold?"
The question is rather when to use heat and when to use cold for any injury. Cold is best in the immediate post-injury period. It inhibits the inflammatory response which follows any injury and lasts about two days. Cold should never precede activity. Heat may help speed the repair process once inflammation has subsided (after about five days). Heat is good before activity as part of a "warm-up" to get the tissues supple and well lubricated. Talk about "increasing circulation" is mostly vague and not well substantiated.

"What is the current medical interpretation of tendonitis and can I prevent it if I already have it? Is the treatment the same for any inflammation?
Tendonitis means inflammation of a tendon. It can also stand in for inflammation of a muscle, joint capsule, bursa, etc. It also usually means abnormal inflammation which has persisted longer than its usual few days after injury, due to continued overuse, improper technique, and numerous other factors.

It is a sad fact that people who have had tendonitis tend to get it again, even with optimum treatment. It can be kept at bay, however, with appropriate stretching, strengthening, attention to technique, and control of excessive zeal. This can be a vexing and delicate, even a trial-and-error, process. Most people require help.

Treatment requires these basic stages: (1) decrease or stop the irritating activities until pain, swelling, tenderness, etc. are gone; (2) wait a bit longer; (3) begin with a specific, deliberate, basic, and progressive exercise; the longer the time and the more systematic this phase, the better; (4) return to activity in a similarly deliberate fashion. Pay lots of attention to technique. Don't overdo it again.

"What are the sports medicine benefits of aspirin? Should I consider cortisone or other steroidal treatments a friend or enemy?"

No drug, given by mouth or needle, is a cure. Both aspirin and "cortisone," as well as the others, act as anti-inflammatory compounds. They can decrease the pain, but they do not repair the damage. In cases of longstanding (chronic) inflammation, the medications can suppress the process to allow healing to begin. By masking pain, they encourage some people to injure themselves further.

"Do certain joints benefit from taping more than others?"

Tape can be used to limit motion in a joint or related structure. It has no use in some joints (shoulder, hip, knee). Taping ankles is quite common to prevent repeat sprains. Athletic training manuals give numerous techniques. In climbing, tape is used to protect the skin and to help support the finger tendons. A wide loop of tape or a Velcro strap around the wide point of the forearm just below the elbow can help limit forearm muscle expansion during use, and benefit tennis elbow sufferers.

"Is weight training really that helpful for preventing injuries?"

Weight training increases strength, which is only one of the determinants of athletic performance. Others include coordination, technique, endurance, balance, flexibility, concentration, experience, etc. As part of a comprehensive program, weight training probably helps avoid injuries by increasing the force which a person can safely use and react to in sports. On the other side, weight lifting produces its own injuries, some quite severe — rotator cuff tears, lumbar disc herniations among them. Overemphasis on this kind of strength — moving considerable fixed poundages around the stationary body — can hamper sports performance. Patrick Edlinger, a rock climbing specialist, is firm on this point. Application of strength in sports usually involves producing or modifying the direction of movement in the body, a process better improved by gymnastics, dance, or similar other movement and balance training methods. These emphasize the use of the internal feedback from the body's own internal movement and position sensors.

"I think I'm overtrained."

Overtraining is much discussed, but not well understood. In its most extreme form, it is a stress syndrome like that experienced by concentration camp inmates: Not enough to eat, too much work, too much mental strain. The result is wasting of the body, the opposite of what training should do. There is depression, loss of protein (muscle), and production of stress hormones. Training to exhaustion too frequently produces this. So can competition. Avoid overtraining by carefully monitoring progress. When progress stops and even greater efforts produce no gain, train less. If training does not seem interesting or exciting, consider this as a possible cause. Extreme cases can be accompanied by weight loss, dark urine, elevated temperature or pulse, or decreased resistance to infection, e.g. frequent colds.

Dr. Robinson suggests the following study list for those wishing to go further into the subject of sports medicine:

"A Window of Healing." John Jerome. *Outside,* May 1985.
"Overuse Injuries." *Clinics in Sports Medicine,* Vol. 5, No. 3, July
    1986.
Sportclimbing: Preparation, Execution, Recovery. Hill, Clune, and
    Robinson. Chockstone Press, 1989.
Exercise Physiology. McArdle, Kuhn, and Kuhn.
Athletic Injuries and Sports Medicine. American Academy of Ortho-
    paedic Surgeons, 1984.
Sports Health. William Soummaya, M.D., 1981.
Sports Medicine. Steven Roy, 1983.

Appendix B:
Glossary of Training Terms
and Abbreviations

Aerobic/Anaerobic: Physiological terms meaning "with oxygen/without oxygen." Like many textbook terms, I find these words misleading and illogical (after all, just how does one go about training "without oxygen"?). I've limited their appearance in this book, relying instead upon the more accurate "CV Training" (Cardiovascular training implies a more holistic and accurate form of "aerobic training"). Basically, aerobic training is doing cardiovascular training like jogging, cycling, etc., at a low to moderate level of intensity. Anaerobic training is cardiovascular training done at near maximum, very high intensity. More simply, while aerobic training, you can converse verbally within the breathing pattern; at anaerobic levels you can't.

alt.: Alternate. As in "Seated Alt. Db. Curls."

bb.: Barbell.

BW: Bodyweight. Usually means to use only one's bodyweight to reach momentary muscular failure as in, say, pullups.

BA: Break Away. I coined this term to mean the process of getting rid of added resistance in a strength-training exercise like Dips, then at bodyweight only, continue until reaching failure. Often seen as "LSBA" meaning "Last Set: Break Away."

CV Training: Cardiovascular training. Activities which strengthen (stress) the heart and its related organs. Examples range from running and cycling, to jumping rope and doing aerobic classes.

db.: Dumbbell(s).

Kinesethetic Training: I use this phrase to generalize activities which enhance total body coordination. This concept illuminates the significance of training in a holistic manner. All movement is the summation of volitional, biomechanical, and emotional factors. To train kinesthetically is to enhance bodily awareness. Such a developed sense of response and control of mind/body/emotional faculties widens and gives depth to an athlete's performance.

LSBA: *See* BA.

LSD: In strength training, this means "Last set, descending." Essentially the act of reducing the resistance to "keep pace" with Momentary Muscular Failure as it occurs. For example: 3x8-10: On the third (final) set, as Failure is reached (about eight reps in this example), the resistance is slightly lightened so as to allow additional repetitions to be performed. This system can be followed in advanced training until the "resistance" cannot be made any lighter (an empty Olympic bar, for example).

In CV Training: Short for "Long, Slow, Distance" aerobic type of training. The principle of "duration" rather than "intensity" is stressed.

MMF: The final climatic point which signals the end of most strength-training sets. Stands for Momentary Muscular Failure. This occurs on the positive (concentric) contraction of the repetition. This is the point at which good form is replaced by extraneous bodily motions which attempt to "assist" the repetition to its top position. Once good technical form has collapsed, MMF has been reached and the set terminated.

Negative Phase: One of the two distinct phases (see Positive Phase) occurring in strength training.

Technically known as an eccentric contraction, the negative phase happens as the muscle cells lengthen (elongate) as tension is created within the muscle.

Positive Phase: One of the two distinct phases (see Negative Phase) occurring in strength training. Commonly referred to as the "explosive phase."

Technically known as concentric contraction, the positive phase happens as the muscle cells shorten (contract) as tension is created within the muscle.

?: This symbol is usually found in the set and repetition schemes of bodyweight exercises such as Dips and Pullups. Just perform the movement it follows until Monentary Muscle Failure is reached; do not add any resistance.

Strength Training: A process by which one educates a progressively greater response from the musculoskeletal system although, like all forms of training, many of the benefits lie outside of pure strength and manifestations.

Superset: A training method in which one alternates exercises successively. For a strength training example:

Do twelve repetitions of a barbell curl;

Do twelve repetitions of a tricep extension.

That is one superset.

Tri Sets: A training technique which follows the same method as in supersets done with three exercises as opposed to two.

(vary): I use this a lot in strength-training program designs. Think of this as a call for creative effort; be open to changing stances, or grip widths. Use different handles, machines, equipment, etc.

WO A/WO B: Used in training prescriptions to indicate a different set and repetition scheme that is to be used alternately during a training cycle. For a strength training example:

Monday: Upper body. Follow sets and reps for WO A.

Tuesday: Lower body. Follow sets and reps for WO A.

Wednesday: Off day.

Thursday: Upper body. Follow sets and reps for WO B.

Friday: Lower body. Follow sets and reps for WO B.

End of cycle; next workout go back to WO A.

x: A symbol meaning "times," as in: 3x8-10 (do three sets times eight to ten repetitions).

Appendix C:
Booklist

Anthony and Thibodeau
Textbook of Anatomy and Physiology. St. Louis, Mo., The C.V. Mosby Company, 1979.

Bergh, Ulf
Physiology of Cross-Country Ski Racing. Champaign, Ill., Human Kinetics Publishers, 1982.

Carlson, Neil R.
Physiology of Behavior. Boston, Mass., Allyn and Bacon, Inc., 1977.

Carrier, Rick and Barbara
Dive. New York, N.Y., Wilfred Funk, Inc., 1955.

Coakley, Jay J.
Sport in Society. St. Louis, Mo., The C.V. Mosby Company, 1982.

Costill, David L.
Inside Running. Indianapolis, Indiana, Benchmark Press, Inc., 1986.

Evans, Jeremy
The Complete Guide to Windsurfing. New York, N.Y., Facts On File Publications, 1983.

Farmer, Charles J.
Canoes, Kayaks, and Rafts. Chicago, Ill.

Fox, Edward L.
Sports Physiology. Philadelphia, Penn., Saunders College Publishing, 1979.

Harris, Dorothy V. and Harris, Bette L.
The Athlete's Guide to Sports Psychology. New York, N.Y., Leisure Press, 1984.

Kahanamoku, Duke.
World of Surfing. New York, N.Y., Grosset & Dunlap, 1968.

Kreutler, Patricia A.
Nutrition in Perspective. Englewood Cliffs, N.J., Prentice-Hall, Inc., 1980.

McCluggage, Denise
The Centered Skier. New York, N.Y., Bantam Books, 1977.

Millman, Dan
The Warrior Athlete. Walpole, N.H., Stillpoint Publishing, 1979.

Pearson, Durk and Shaw, Sandy
Life Extension. New York, N.Y., Warner Books, 1982.

Radcliffe, James C.
Plyometrics. Champaign, Ill., Human Kinetics Publishers, Inc., 1985.

Schad, Jerry
Adventure Running. South Bend, Indiana, Icarus Press, 1983.

Sharkey, David J.
Physiology of Fitness. Champaign, Ill., Human Kinetics Publishers, Inc., 1979

Sheehan, George
This Running Life. New York, N.Y., Simon & Schuster, 1980.

Swift, Sally
Centered Riding. North Pomfret, Vermont, David & Charles, Inc., 1985.

Weider, Joe
Bodybuilding. Chicago, Ill., Contemporary Books, 1981.

Wells, Christine L.
Women, Sport & Performance. Champaign, Ill., Human Kinetics Publishers, 1985.

Wirhed, Rolf
Athletic Ability. AB Orebro, Sweden, Harpoon Publications, 1984.

Index

A Word About the Training Journal...

Steve Ilg's THE OUTDOOR ATHLETE'S TRAINING JOURNAL is a twelve-month cross-training guide for wholistic fitness and sport performance. It includes your twelve-month journal for personal record-keeping, a yearly logbook to summarize your progress, and Steve's monthly essays to focus your training and encourage your performance. The journal is undated so that you may start today!

To reach Steve Ilg with questions about a training program tailored to your specific needs, please write or call Cordillera Press, Inc., P.O. Box 3699, Evergreen, Colorado 80439, (303) 670-3010. To order your copy of THE OUTDOOR ATHLETE'S TRAINING JOURNAL, or additional copies of THE OUTDOOR ATHLETE, please send $14.95 per book, plus $2.00 postage for the first book and $1.00 for each additional book ordered, to Cordillera Press at the above address.